WORD by WORD

ワード・バイ・ワード イラスト辞典

日本語併記版

Steven J. Molinsky　Bill Bliss

ピアソン

Acquisitions editor: *Tina Carver*
Managing editor, production:
Production editor: *Janet Johnston*
Electronic production technology coordinator:
Electronic production: *Steven K. Jorgensen*
Interior design: *Kenny Beck*
Cover supervisor: *Marianne Frasco*
Cover design: *Merle Krumper*
Buyer/scheduler: *Ray Keating*

Illustrated by RICHARD E. HILL

Printed in Japan

ISBN4-89471-802-2

『ワード・バイ・ワード イラスト辞典』では、3,000 語以上の単語を生き生きとした楽しいイラストの中で紹介しています。各ページには各単語を用いて使える会話文（ダイアログ）を掲載し、学習者が日常の様々な状況において効果的にコミュニケーションを行うために即必要な単語の学習を促します。また、この二ケ国語版では、日本語を併記しておりイラストではもちろんのこと日本語でも英語の意味を確認することができます。(可能な限り日本語訳を左側に併記し、訳を隠しても使えるようにつくられています)

『ワード・バイ・ワード』では、単語は100のテーマに分類され、それぞれについて単語の意味だけでなく、学習者が即使うことができる簡単な例文から会話一般にいたるまで幅広いレッスンが提供されています。前半の課では[家族]や［家］について、そしてその後に続く課では［日常生活の動作]、[地域社会]、[学校]、[職場]、[買物]、[レクリエーション]などについてカバーしています。また、『ワード・バイ・ワード』 は日常重要となる生活スキルを幅広く包括し、学校の教科や課外活動における単語等も収録しています。そして、各課はそれぞれ独立していますので、最初の課から順番に使っても、好きな課から始めても使えます。

ご使用になる方の便宜を図り、ワード・バイ・ワードは2通りの索引を掲載しています。１つは、ページ順の［目次]、そしてもう1つがアルファベット順にした[項目別索引]です。これらを巻末付録の単語索引とあわせて使えば、お使いの学習者や先生が容易に単語トピックをこのイラスト辞典の中で見つけることができます。
ワード・バイ・ワード イラスト辞典は様々なレベルに対応できる「ワード・バイ・ワード単語増強コース」の中心となるテキストです。この日本語併記の二ケ国語版、そして本書のオリジナルでもある英語版テキストの他に、3レベルのワークブック (Literacy, Beginning, Intermediate)、先生用リソースブック(Teacher's Resource Book & Activities Masters)、ボキャブラリー教授戦略ハンドブック (Handbook of Vocabulary Teaching Strategies)、オーディオ・テープ、ウォール・チャート、カラーOHPシート(Transparencies)、ゲームカード、ソング・アルバム、ソング・ブック、テスト・プログラムとシリーズの構成も充実しています。

教科書として使用される先生方へーその教授戦略ー

『ワード・バイ・ワード』は単語を文脈の中で紹介しているこれまでにない画期的なピクチャー・ディクショナリーです。各ページのモデル・カンバセーション（会話例文）は、その単語が実際のコミュニケーションの中で使われる状況を提示しています。この例文を基礎にして学習単語を生き生きとした会話の中で用い、学習者同士が相互的に習得していくことを可能としました。また、各課には簡単なライティング及びディスカッションの質問項目を設け、学習者が自分自身や文化について、自分の経験、考え、意見、情報などを分かち合いながら、各課の単語やテーマを自分の生活に関連づけて理解できるように配慮されています。こうして学習者は文字通り“単語ごとに (word by word)” それぞれを習得していきます。

『ワード・バイ・ワード』を使いながら、生徒のニーズや能力、そして先生ご自身の教授法にあったアプローチや教授戦略を開発されることをおすすめします。各課の単語を紹介し練習する上で、お役に立ちそうな教授テクニック法を下記に紹介しています。ご参考下さい。

1. 単語のプレビューイング：ウォームアップとして、学習する前に生徒がすでに知っている単語等があればそれらをうまく引き出していく。その課の単語をブレーンストーミング的に生徒に当てさせてみる／黒板に書き出す／付属のウォール・チャート、OHPシート、テキストのイラストを見せる等、これらのアクティビティを行って生徒がよく知っている単語を認識する。

2. 単語の提示：まず各単語のイラストを指摘し、単語を先生が口に出して紹介する。その後クラス全体または一人一人で単語を復唱させる。生徒が各単語の意味を理解し、発音していることを確認する。

3. 単語演習：クラス全体で、ペアで、または小グループで生徒に単語演習をさせる。先生が単語を口に出すか、書き出し、その後生徒にその単語をあらわしているイラストを指摘させるか番号を言わせる。また、逆に先生がイラストを指摘するか、番号をあげその後生徒に単語を言わせる。

4. モデル・カンバセーション演習：モデル・カンバセーション（会話例文）の箇所において用いられている単語は、その課の単語リスト上最初に出てくる単語であるか、または単語を入れかえられるようその単語の部分は下線が引かれ空欄になっている。空欄の場合、[ ] 内に示された数字の単語を例文に用いることが可能。また、[ ] のついた数字が例文に示されていなければ、そのページの単語すべてをあてはめることが可能。

モデル・カンバセーション演習では、次のステップですすめていくことをおすすめします。

a. プレビュー：生徒にモデルとなっている例文脇のイラストを見せ、生徒にその会話はだれが話しているのか、どこでその会話がなされているのかを考えさせ、ディスカッションをさせる。

b. 例文を提示し、生徒がその会話の状況と単語の意味を理解していることを確かめる。

c. 会話の各文をクラス全体で、または生徒一人一人で復唱させる。

d. モデル・ダイアログを生徒同士ペアで練習させる。

e. ペアとなった生徒一組に、例文に基づいた新しい会話を発表させる。その際単語リストに載っている別の単語を使わせる。

f. 生徒同士ペアを組ませ、例文に基づいた新しい会話を数文練習させる。その際それまでに未使用の単語を用いる。

g. 何組かのペアに自分たちがつくった会話をクラスで発表させる。

5. 補足会話演習：リスト内の単語を用いた会話演習の発展として、多課に渡り空所補充形式の補足会話文をそれぞれ２つ掲載している。（ページ下の黄色い部分）。生徒にこれらの例文を練習させ、その後使いたい単語を例文にあてはめて発表させる。

6. ライティング及びスペリング演習：クラス全体で、ペアで、または小グループで単語のスペリング演習を行う。先生が単語を言うか、単語の綴りを口に出して言い、生徒にその単語を書きとらせ、その単語のイラストを指摘させるか番号を言わせる。または、逆に先生がイラストを指すか番号を言い、生徒にその単語を書かせる。

7. ディスカッション、作文、日記、生徒の作品集としてのテーマ：『ワード・バイ・ワード』では各課にディスカッション、作文のための質問が１つ以上掲載されている(ページ下の緑色の部分)。クラス全体で、ペアで、または小グループで生徒にその質問に対して応えさせる。または、それらを宿題として書かせたり、その作文を他の生徒と交換させたりし、その後クラス全体で、ペアで、または小グループでディスカッションを行ってみる。

書いた作文を日記として残していくのもまた楽しく学習する一つの方法といえる。 時間に余裕があるなら、各生徒の日記を読み、生徒の書いたことに応えるだけではなく、先生自身の意見や経験を書き加えてみるのもよいかもしれない。

また、生徒の作品を成果記録としてとっている先生方にとって、これらの作文は生徒の英語学習の進歩度を計る最高の資料にもなりえる。

8. コミュニケーション・アクティビティ：「ワード・バイ・ワード先生用リソースブック」は多彩なゲーム、タスクベース演習、ブレーンストーミング、ディスカッション、絵描き、ジェスチャー、ロールプレイなど多様なアクティビティを収録しており、先生の様々なレベルや能力、学習スタイルにうまく対応できるよう設定されている。このリソースブックから各課に対し１つか２つぐらいのアクティビティを選び、その生徒の意欲を高めるクリエイティブかつ楽しい手法で生徒の単語学習を強化していく。

ワード・バイ・ワードは、生徒のコミュニケーション能力を高めながら、意味のある、そして生き生きとした英単語演習を提供することを目的としています。私たちがつくったこのコースの本質を伝える上で、私たちが信じる教育理念も今ここでご理解いただけましたら誠に幸いです。この理念とは、すなわち単語学習は生徒自らによる真の相互コミュニケーションであるべきで、生徒の生活に密接に関連し、生徒の能力や学習スタイルにどのようにでも対応でき、そして何よりも楽しくあるべきである、ということです。

スティーブン・J・モリンスキー
ビル ・ ブリス

（日本ELT編集部訳）

A. What's your **name**?
B. *Nancy Ann Peterson.*

APPLICATION

Name (1): Nancy (2) first — Ann (3) middle — Peterson (4) last
Address (5): 42 (6) number — Main Street (7) street — #5A (8) apt.
Long Beach, (9) city — CA (10) state — 22960 (11) zip code
Telephone: (213) (12) 684-1196 (13)
SSN: 045-61-8947 (14)

名前 **1.** name
名 **2.** first name
ミドルネーム **3.** middle name
名字 **4.** last name/family name/surname

住所 **5.** address
番地 **6.** street number
通り（町）**7.** street
住宅番号 **8.** apartment number
市 **9.** city

州 **10.** state
郵便番号 **11.** zip code
市外局番 **12.** area code
電話番号 **13.** telephone number/phone number
社会保障番号 **14.** Social Security Number

A. What's your ________?
B. ....
A. Did you say ....?
B. Yes. That's right.

A. What's your last name?
B. ....
A. How do you spell that?
B. ....

Tell about yourself:
My name is ....
My address is ....
My telephone number is ....
Now interview a friend.

A. Who is she?
B. She's my **wife**.
A. What's her name?

A. Who is he?
B. He's my **husband**.
A. What's his name?

妻 **1.** wife
夫 **2.** husband

両親 **parents**
母 **3.** mother
父 **4.** father

子供 **children**
娘 **5.** daughter
息子 **6.** son
姉/妹 **7.** sister
兄/弟 **8.** brother
赤ん坊 **9.** baby

祖父母 **grandparents**
祖母 **10.** grandmother
祖父 **11.** grandfather

孫 **grandchildren**
孫娘 **12.** granddaughter
孫息子 **13.** grandson

A. I'd like to introduce my _______.
B. Nice to meet you.
C. Nice to meet you, too.

A. What's your _______'s name?
B. His/Her name is ....

Tell about your family.
Talk about photos of family members.

A. Who is she?
B. She's my **aunt**.
A. What's her name?

A. Who is he?
B. He's my **uncle**.
A. What's his name?

おば **1.** aunt
おじ **2.** uncle
めい **3.** niece
おい **4.** nephew

いとこ **5.** cousin
義母 **6.** mother-in-law
義父 **7.** father-in-law
義理の息子 **8.** son-in-law

義理の娘 **9.** daughter-in-law
義理の兄/弟 **10.** brother-in-law
義理の姉/妹 **11.** sister-in-law

A. Is he/she your ________?
B. No. He's/She's my ________.
A. Oh. What's his/her name?
B. …………

A. Let me introduce my ________.
B. I'm glad to meet you.
C. Nice meeting you, too.

Tell about your relatives:
What are their names?
Where do they live?
Draw your family tree and talk about it.

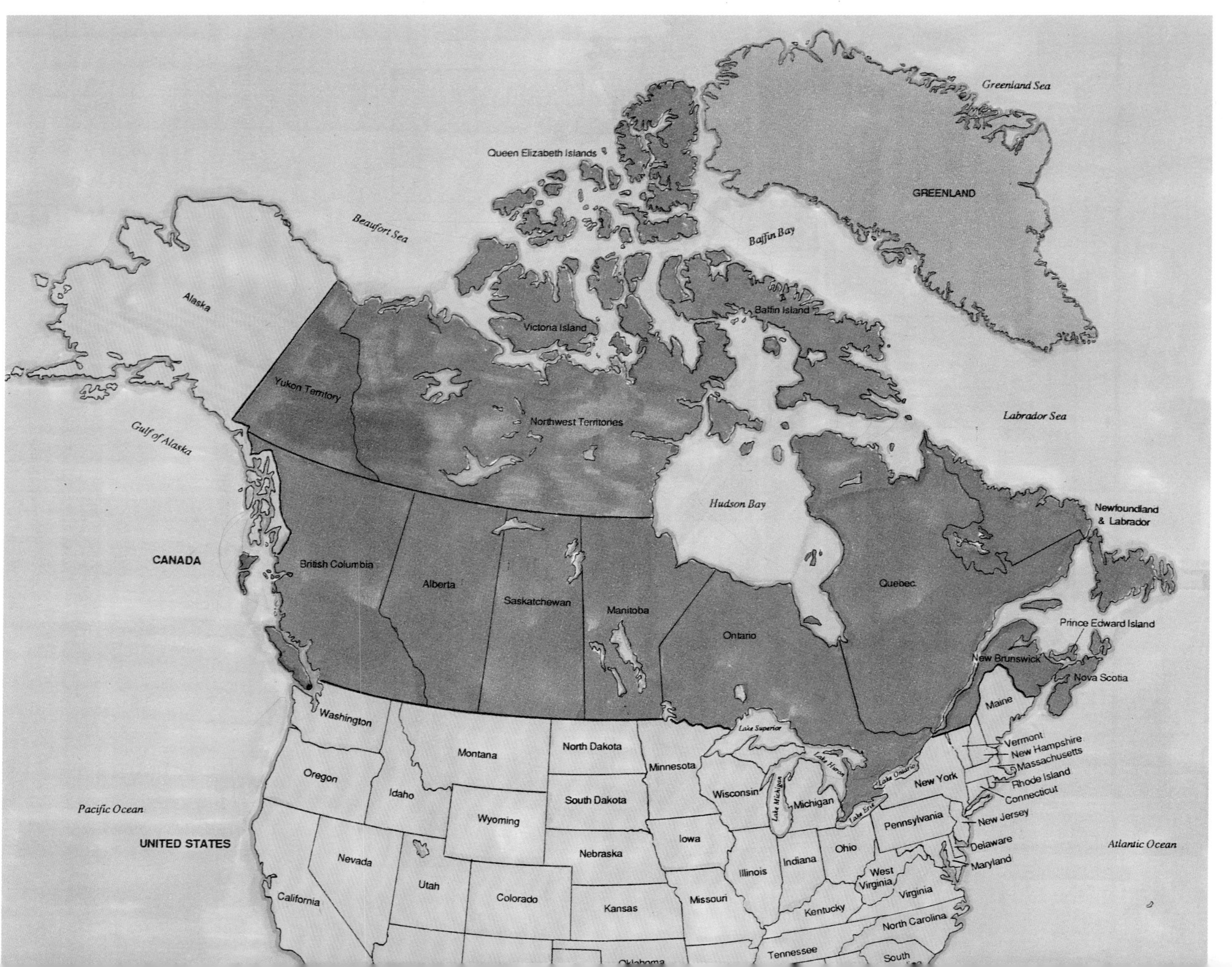
Greenland Sea
GREENLAND
Queen Elizabeth Islands
Beaufort Sea
Baffin Bay
Alaska
Victoria Island
Baffin Island
Yukon Territory
Northwest Territories
Labrador Sea
Gulf of Alaska
Hudson Bay
Newfoundland
& Labrador
CANADA
British Columbia
Alberta
Saskatchewan
Manitoba
Quebec
Ontario
Prince Edward Island
New Brunswick
Nova Scotia
Maine
Washington
Montana
North Dakota
Lake Superior
Minnesota
Lake Huron
Lake Ontario
Vermont
New Hampshire
Massachusetts
Oregon
New York
Rhode Island
Wisconsin
Lake Michigan
Michigan
Connecticut
Idaho
South Dakota
Lake Erie
Pacific Ocean
Wyoming
Pennsylvania
New Jersey
UNITED STATES
Iowa
Nebraska
Delaware
Atlantic Ocean
Nevada
Ohio
Maryland
Illinois
Indiana
West
Virginia
Utah
Colorado
Virginia
California
Missouri
Kansas
Kentucky
North Carolina
Tennessee
Oklahoma
South

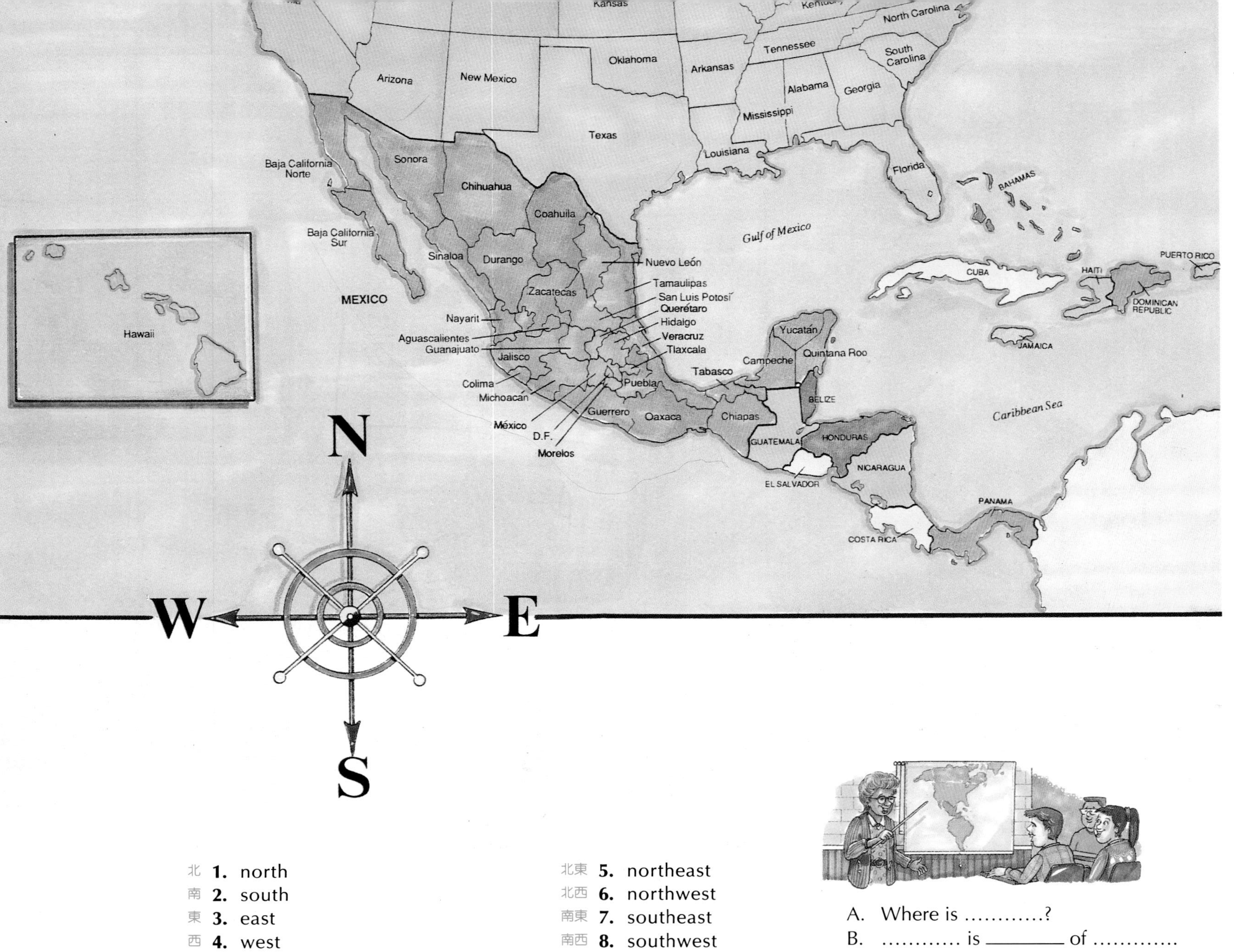

北 **1.** north
南 **2.** south
東 **3.** east
西 **4.** west

北東 **5.** northeast
北西 **6.** northwest
南東 **7.** southeast
南西 **8.** southwest

A. Where is ....?
B. .... is ________ of ....

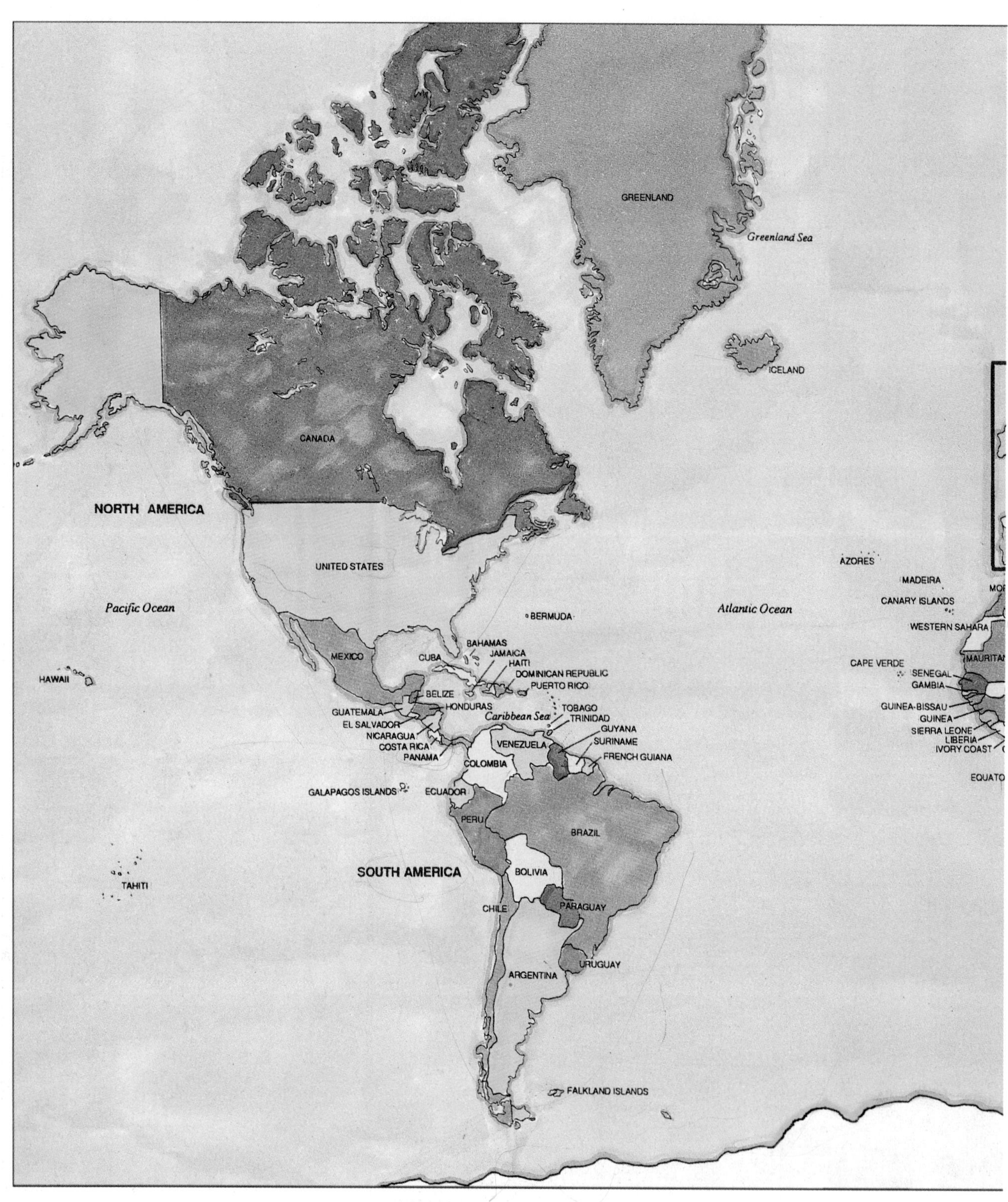

北アメリカ **1.** North America
南アメリカ **2.** South America
ヨーロッパ **3.** Europe
アフリカ **4.** Africa
中東 **5.** The Middle East
アジア **6.** Asia
オーストラリア **7.** Australia
南極 **8.** Antarctica

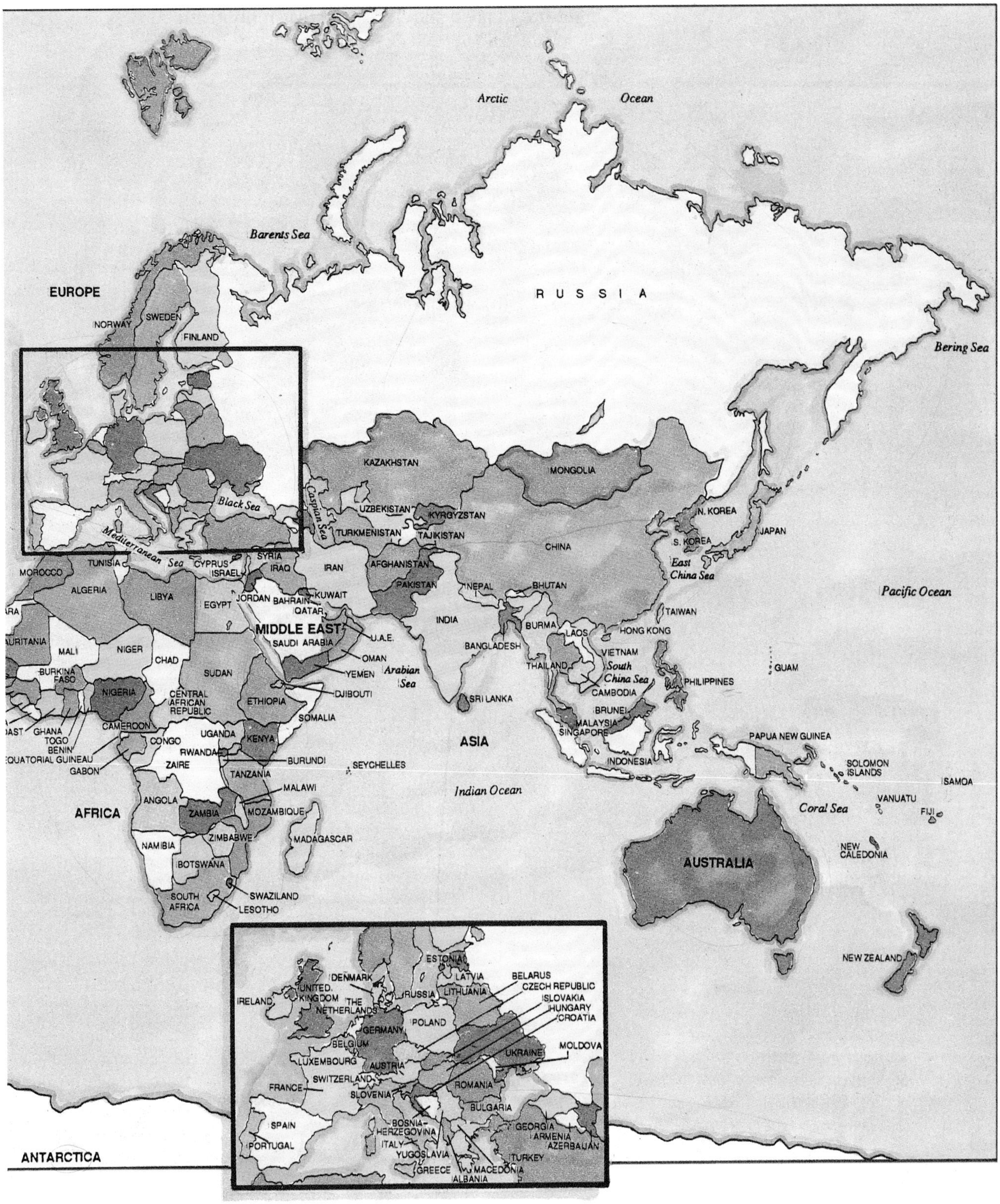

A. Where's ....?
B. It's in ________.

A. What ocean/sea is near ....?
B. The .... Ocean/Sea.

A. What do you do every day?
B. I **get up**, I **take a shower**, and I **brush my teeth**.

起床する **1.** get up
シャワーを浴びる **2.** take a shower
歯をみがく **3.** brush *my** teeth
歯間そうじをする **4.** floss *my** teeth
ひげをそる **5.** shave
服を着る **6.** get dressed
顔を洗う **7.** wash *my** face

化粧をする **8.** put on makeup
髪をブラシでとかす **9.** brush *my** hair
髪をくしでとかす **10.** comb *my** hair
ベッドを整える **11.** make the bed
服を脱ぐ **12.** get undressed
風呂に入る **13.** take a bath
床につく **14.** go to bed

眠る **15.** sleep
朝食を作る **16.** make breakfast
昼食を作る **17.** make lunch
夕食を作る **18.** cook/make dinner
朝食を食べる **19.** eat/have breakfast
昼食を食べる **20.** eat/have lunch
夕食を食べる **21.** eat/have dinner

*私の，彼の，私達の，あなた(達)の，彼(女)らの　*my,his,our,your,their

A. What does he do every day?
B. He ________s, he ________s, and he ________s.

A. What does she do every day?
B. She ________s, she ________s, and she ________s.

What do you do every day? Make a list.
Interview some friends and tell about their everyday activities.

A. Hi! What are you doing?
B. I'm **clean**ing **the apartment**.

家の掃除をする **1.** clean the apartment/ clean the house
床を掃く **2.** sweep the floor
ほこりを払う **3.** dust
掃除機をかける **4.** vacuum
皿を洗う **5.** wash the dishes
洗濯をする **6.** do the laundry

アイロンをかける **7.** iron
赤ちゃんに食事をさせる **8.** feed the baby
ネコにえさを与える **9.** feed the cat
犬を散歩させる **10.** walk the dog
テレビをみる **11.** watch TV
ラジオを聞く **12.** listen to the radio
音楽を聞く **13.** listen to music

読書する **14.** read
遊ぶ **15.** play
バスケットボールをする **16.** play basketball
ギターを弾く **17.** play the guitar
ピアノの練習をする **18.** practice the piano
勉強する **19.** study
運動する **20.** exercise

A. Hi, ...! This is .... What are you doing?
B. I'm ________ing. How about you?
A. I'm ________ing.

A. Are you going to ________ today?
B. Yes. I'm going to ________ in a little while.

What are you going to do tomorrow? Make a list of *everything* you are going to do.

A. Where's the **teacher**?
B. The **teacher** is *next to* the **board**.

A. Where's the **pen**?
B. The **pen** is *on* the **desk**.

先生	**1.**	teacher
助手	**2.**	teacher's aide
生徒	**3.**	student
いす	**4.**	seat/chair
ペン	**5.**	pen
鉛筆	**6.**	pencil
消しゴム	**7.**	eraser
机	**8.**	desk
教卓	**9.**	teacher's desk
教科書	**10.**	book/textbook
ノート	**11.**	notebook
ノート用紙	**12.**	notebook paper
方眼紙	**13.**	graph paper
ものさし	**14.**	ruler
電卓	**15.**	calculator
時計	**16.**	clock
旗	**17.**	flag
黒板	**18.**	board
チョーク	**19.**	chalk
チョーク入れ	**20.**	chalk tray
黒板消し	**21.**	eraser
スピーカー	**22.**	P.A. system/ loudspeaker
掲示板	**23.**	bulletin board
画びょう	**24.**	thumbtack
地図	**25.**	map
鉛筆削り	**26.**	pencil sharpener
地球儀	**27.**	globe
本棚	**28.**	bookshelf
オーバーヘッド・プロジェクター	**29.**	overhead projector
テレビ	**30.**	TV
スクリーン	**31.**	(movie) screen
スライド映写機	**32.**	slide projector
コンピューター	**33.**	computer
映写機	**34.**	(movie) projector

A. Is there a/an ________ in your classroom?*
B. Yes. There's a/an ________ next to/on the ________.

A. Is there a/an ________ in your classroom?*
B. No, there isn't.

With 12, 13, 19 use: Is there ________ in your classroom?

Describe your classroom.
(There's a/an ....)

Practice these classroom actions.

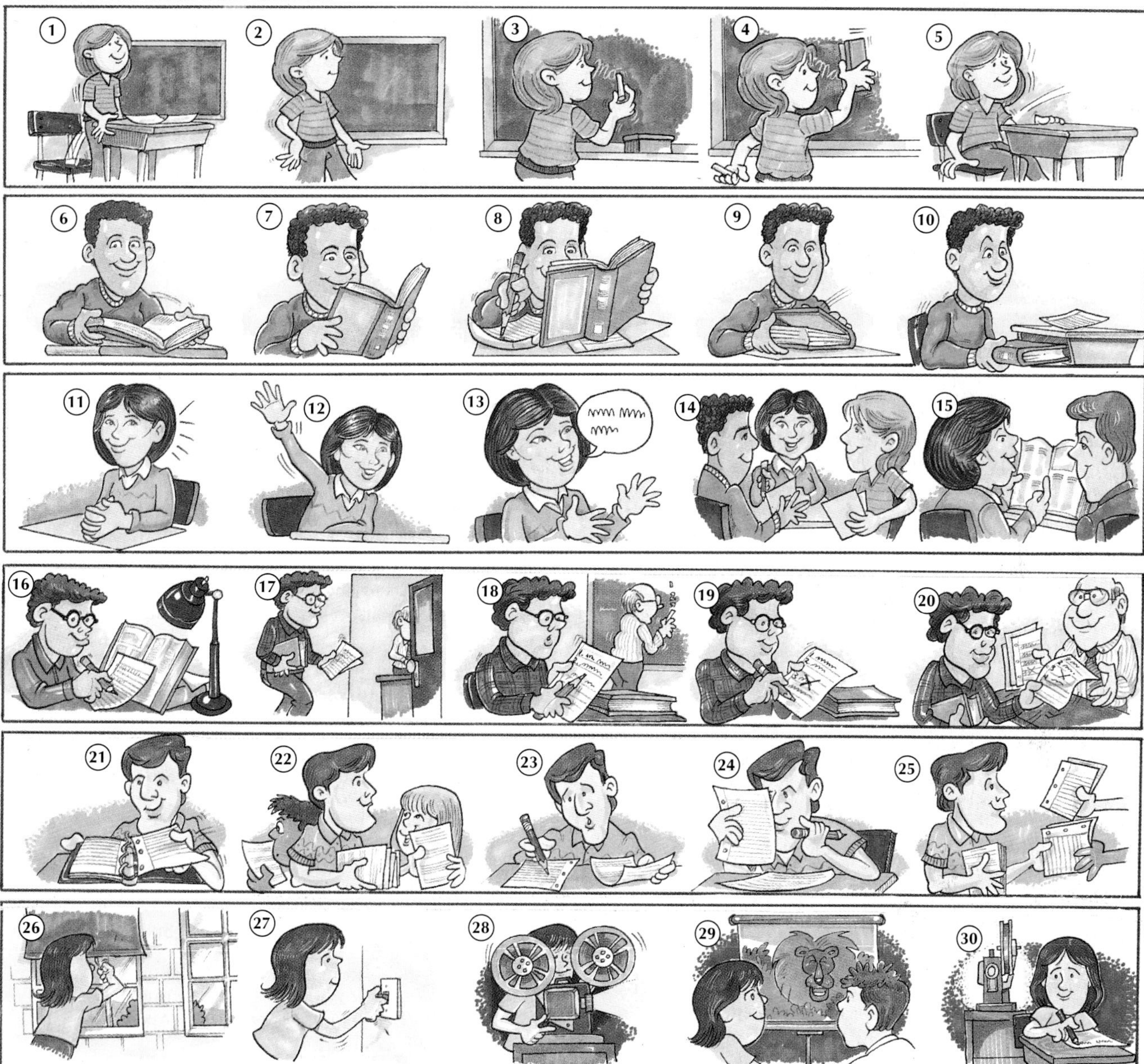

立ちなさい。	**1.** Stand up.
黒板のところへ行きなさい。	**2.** Go to *the board*.
名前を書きなさい。	**3.** Write *your name*.
名前を消しなさい。	**4.** Erase *your name*.
席に着きなさい。	**5.** Sit down./Take your seat.
本を開けなさい。	**6.** Open *your book*.
8ページを読みなさい。	**7.** Read *page eight*.
8ページを学習しなさい。	**8.** Study *page eight*.
本を閉じなさい。	**9.** Close *your book*.
本を片づけなさい。	**10.** Put away *your book*.
質問を聞きなさい。	**11.** Listen to *the question*.
手をあげなさい。	**12.** Raise *your hand*.
答えを言いなさい。	**13.** Give *the answer*.
グループで学習しなさい。	**14.** Work *in groups*.
お互いに助け合いなさい。	**15.** Help *each other*.
宿題をして来なさい。	**16.** Do *your homework*.
宿題を持って来なさい。	**17.** Bring in *your homework*.
答えあわせをしなさい。	**18.** Go over *the answers*.
誤りを正しなさい。	**19.** Correct *your mistakes*.
宿題を提出しなさい。	**20.** Hand in *your homework*.
紙を1枚取り出しなさい。	**21.** Take out *a piece of paper*.
テストを配りなさい。	**22.** Pass out *the tests*.
問いに答えなさい。	**23.** Answer *the questions*.
答えを確かめなさい。	**24.** Check *your answers*.
テストを集めなさい。	**25.** Collect *the tests*.
ブラインドを下ろしなさい。	**26.** Lower *the shades*.
電気を消しなさい。	**27.** Turn off *the lights*.
映写機をまわしなさい。	**28.** Turn on *the projector*.
映画を見なさい。	**29.** Watch *the movie*.
メモを取りなさい。	**30.** Take notes.

You're the teacher! Give instructions to your students.

A. Where are you from?
B. I'm from **Mexico**.

A. What's your nationality?
B. I'm **Mexican**.

A. What language do you speak?
B. I speak **Spanish**.

  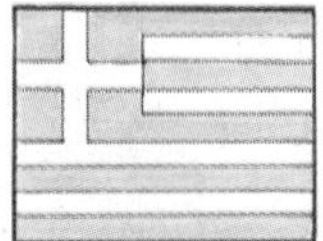   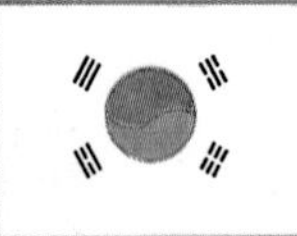 

Country 国	Nationality 国籍	Language 言語
Afghanistan アフガニスタン	Afghan アフガニスタン人	Afghan アフガニスタン語
Argentina アルゼンチン	Argentine アルゼンチン人	Spanish スペイン語
Australia オーストラリア	Australian オーストラリア人	English 英語
Bolivia ボリビア	Bolivian ボリビア人	Spanish スペイン語
Brazil ブラジル	Brazilian ブラジル人	Portuguese ポルトガル語
Cambodia カンボジア	Cambodian カンボジア人	Cambodian カンボジア語(クメール語)
Canada カナダ	Canadian カナダ人	English/French 英語/フランス語
Chile チリ	Chilean チリ人	Spanish スペイン語
China 中国	Chinese 中国人	Chinese 中国語
Colombia コロンビア	Colombian コロンビア人	Spanish スペイン語
Costa Rica コスタリカ	Costa Rican コスタリカ人	Spanish スペイン語
Cuba キューバ	Cuban キューバ人	Spanish スペイン語
(The) Dominican Republic ドミニカ共和国	Dominican ドミニカ人	Spanish スペイン語
Ecuador エクアドル	Ecuadorian エクアドル人	Spanish スペイン語
Egypt エジプト	Egyptian エジプト人	Arabic アラビア語
El Salvador エルサルバドル	Salvadorean エルサルバドル人	Spanish スペイン語
England イギリス	English イギリス人	English 英語
Estonia エストニア	Estonian エストニア人	Estonian エストニア語
Ethiopia エチオピア	Ethiopian エチオピア人	Amharic アムハラ語
France フランス	French フランス人	French フランス語
Germany ドイツ	German ドイツ人	German ドイツ語
Greece ギリシア	Greek ギリシア人	Greek ギリシア語
Guatemala グアテマラ	Guatemalan グアテマラ人	Spanish スペイン語
Hungary ハンガリー	Hungarian ハンガリー人	Hungarian ハンガリー語
Honduras ホンジュラス	Honduran ホンジュラス人	Spanish スペイン語

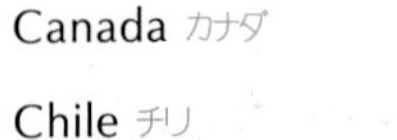

Country 国	Nationality 国籍	Language 言語
Indonesia インドネシア	Indonesian インドネシア人	Indonesian インドネシア語
Israel イスラエル	Israeli イスラエル人	Hebrew ヘブライ語
Italy イタリア	Italian イタリア人	Italian イタリア語
Japan 日本	Japanese 日本人	Japanese 日本語
Jordan ヨルダン	Jordanian ヨルダン人	Arabic アラビア語
Korea 韓国/朝鮮	Korean 韓国人/朝鮮人	Korean 韓国語/朝鮮語
Laos ラオス	Laotian ラオス人	Laotian ラオス語
Latvia ラトビア	Latvian ラトビア人	Latvian ラトビア語
Lithuania リトアニア	Lithuanian リトアニア人	Lithuanian リトアニア語
Malaysia マレーシア	Malaysian マレーシア人	Malay マライ語
Mexico メキシコ	Mexican メキシコ人	Spanish スペイン語
New Zealand ニュージーランド	New Zealander ニュージーランド人	English 英語
Nicaragua ニカラグア	Nicaraguan ニカラグア人	Spanish スペイン語
Panama パナマ	Panamanian パナマ人	Spanish スペイン語
Peru ペルー	Peruvian ペルー人	Spanish スペイン語
(The) Philippines フィリピン	Filipino フィリピン人	Tagalog タガログ語
Poland ポーランド	Polish ポーランド人	Polish ポーランド語
Portugal ポルトガル	Portuguese ポルトガル人	Portuguese ポルトガル語
Puerto Rico プエルトリコ	Puerto Rican プエルトリコ人	Spanish スペイン語
Romania ルーマニア	Romanian ルーマニア人	Romanian ルーマニア語
Russia ロシア	Russian ロシア人	Russian ロシア語
Saudi Arabia サウジアラビア	Saudi サウジアラビア人	Arabic アラビア語
Spain スペイン	Spanish スペイン人	Spanish スペイン語
Taiwan 台湾	Taiwanese 台湾人	Chinese 中国語
Thailand タイ	Thai タイ人	Thai タイ語
Turkey トルコ	Turkish トルコ人	Turkish トルコ語
Ukraine ウクライナ	Ukrainian ウクライナ人	Ukrainian ウクライナ語
(The) United アメリカ合衆国	American アメリカ人	English 英語
Venezuela ベネズエラ	Venezuelan ベネズエラ人	Spanish スペイン語
Vietnam ベトナム	Vietnamese ベトナム人	Vietnamese ベトナム語

 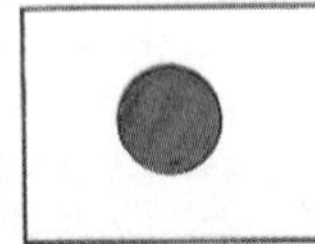     

A. What's your native language?
B. _______.
A. Oh. What country are you from?
B. _______.

A. Where are you and your husband/wife going on your vacation?
B. We're going to _______.
A. That's nice. Tell me, do you speak _______?
B. No, but my husband/wife does. He's/She's _______.

Tell about yourself:
- Where are you from?
- What's your nationality?
- What languages do you speak?

Now interview and tell about a friend.

A. Where do you live?
B. I live in an **apartment building**.

アパート（賃貸の集合住宅） **1.** apartment (building)
一戸建て住宅 **2.** (single-family) house
二世帯用住宅 **3.** duplex/two-family house
連棟住宅 **4.** townhouse/townhome
（分譲）マンション **5.** condominium/condo
寮 **6.** dormitory/dorm
モービルホーム/トレーラーハウス **7.** mobile home/trailer
農家 **8.** farmhouse
小屋 **9.** cabin
養老院 **10.** nursing home
避難所/保護施設 **11.** shelter
ハウスボート（家船） **12.** houseboat

A. Town Taxi Company.
B. Hello. Please send a taxi to *(address)*.
A. Is that a house or an apartment?
B. It's a/an ________.
A. All right. We'll be there right away.

A. This is the Emergency Operator.
B. Please send an ambulance to *(address)*.
A. Is that a private home?
B. It's a/an ________.
A. What's your name?
B. ....
A. And your telephone number?
B. ....

Tell about people you know and the types of housing they live in.

Discuss:
Who lives in dormitories?
Who lives in nursing homes?
Who lives in shelters?
Why?

A. Where are you?
B. I'm in the living room.
A. What are you doing?
B. I'm *dusting** the **coffee table**.

*dusting/cleaning

- センターテーブル **1.** coffee table
- じゅうたん **2.** rug
- 床 **3.** floor
- ひじ掛けいす **4.** armchair
- サイドテーブル **5.** end table
- ランプ **6.** lamp
- ランプのかさ **7.** lampshade
- 窓 **8.** window
- カーテン **9.** drapes/ curtains
- ソファ **10.** sofa/couch
- クッション **11.** (throw)pillow
- 天井 **12.** ceiling
- 壁 **13.** wall
- 飾り棚 **14.** wall unit/ entertainment unit
- テレビ **15.** television
- ビデオデッキ **16.** video cassette recorder/VCR
- ステレオ **17.** stereo system
- スピーカー **18.** speaker
- 2人掛けソファ **19.** loveseat
- （観葉）植物 **20.** plant
- 絵 **21.** painting
- 額 **22.** frame
- マントル（炉棚） **23.** mantle
- 暖炉 **24.** fireplace
- 暖炉ガード **25.** fireplace screen
- 写真 **26.** picture/ photograph
- 本箱 **27.** bookcase

A. You have a lovely living room!
B. Oh, thank you.
A. Your ________ is/are beautiful!
B. Thank you for saying so.

A. Uh-oh! I just spilled coffee on your ________!
B. That's okay. Don't worry about it.

Tell about your living room.
(In my living room there's ....)

A. This **dining room table** is very nice.
B. Thank you. It was a gift from my *grandmother.**
*grandmother/grandfather/aunt/uncle/...

- 食卓 **1.** (dining room) table
- いす **2.** (dining room) chair
- 食器棚 **3.** china cabinet
- 陶磁器 **4.** china
- シャンデリア **5.** chandelier
- サイドボード **6.** buffet
- サラダボウル **7.** salad bowl
- 水さし **8.** pitcher
- 配ぜん用の大ボウル **9.** serving bowl
- 配ぜん用の大皿 **10.** serving platter
- テーブルクロス **11.** tablecloth
- 燭台 **12.** candlestick
- ろうそく **13.** candle
- テーブルセンター **14.** centerpiece
- 塩入れ **15.** salt shaker
- こしょう入れ **16.** pepper shaker
- バター入れ **17.** butter dish
- (配ぜん用) ワゴン **18.** serving cart
- ティーポット **19.** teapot
- コーヒーポット **20.** coffee pot
- クリーム入れ **21.** creamer
- 砂糖入れ **22.** sugar bowl

[In a store]

A. May I help you?
B. Yes, please. Do you have ________s?*
A. Yes. ________s* are right over there.
B. Thank you.

**With 4, use the singular.*

[At home]

A. Look at this old ________ I just bought!
B. Where did you buy it?
A. At a yard sale. How do you like it?
B. It's VERY unusual!

Tell about your dining room.
(In my dining room there's ....)

A. Excuse me. Where does the **salad plate** go?
B. It goes *to the left of* the **dinner plate**.

A. Excuse me. Where does the **soup spoon** go?
B. It goes *to the right of* the **teaspoon**.

A. Excuse me. Where does the **wine glass** go?
B. It goes *between* the **water glass** and the **cup and saucer**.

A. Excuse me. Where does the **cup** go?
B. It goes *on* the **saucer**.

サラダ皿 **1.** salad plate
パン皿 **2.** bread-and-butter plate
ディナー皿（飾り皿） **3.** dinner plate
スープ皿 **4.** soup bowl
水用グラス **5.** water glass
ワイングラス **6.** wine glass
カップ **7.** cup
受け皿 **8.** saucer
ナプキン **9.** napkin

銀食器 **silverware**

サラダフォーク **10.** salad fork
フォーク **11.** dinner fork
ナイフ **12.** knife
ティースプーン **13.** teaspoon
スープスプーン **14.** soup spoon
バターナイフ **15.** butter knife

A. Waiter? Excuse me. This ________ is dirty.
B. I'm terribly sorry. I'll get you another ________ right away.

A. Oops! I dropped my ________!
B. That's okay! I'll get you another ________ from the kitchen.

Practice giving directions. Tell someone how to set a table. (Put the ....)

A. Ooh! Look at that big bug!!
B. Where?
A. It's on the **bed**!
B. I'LL get it.

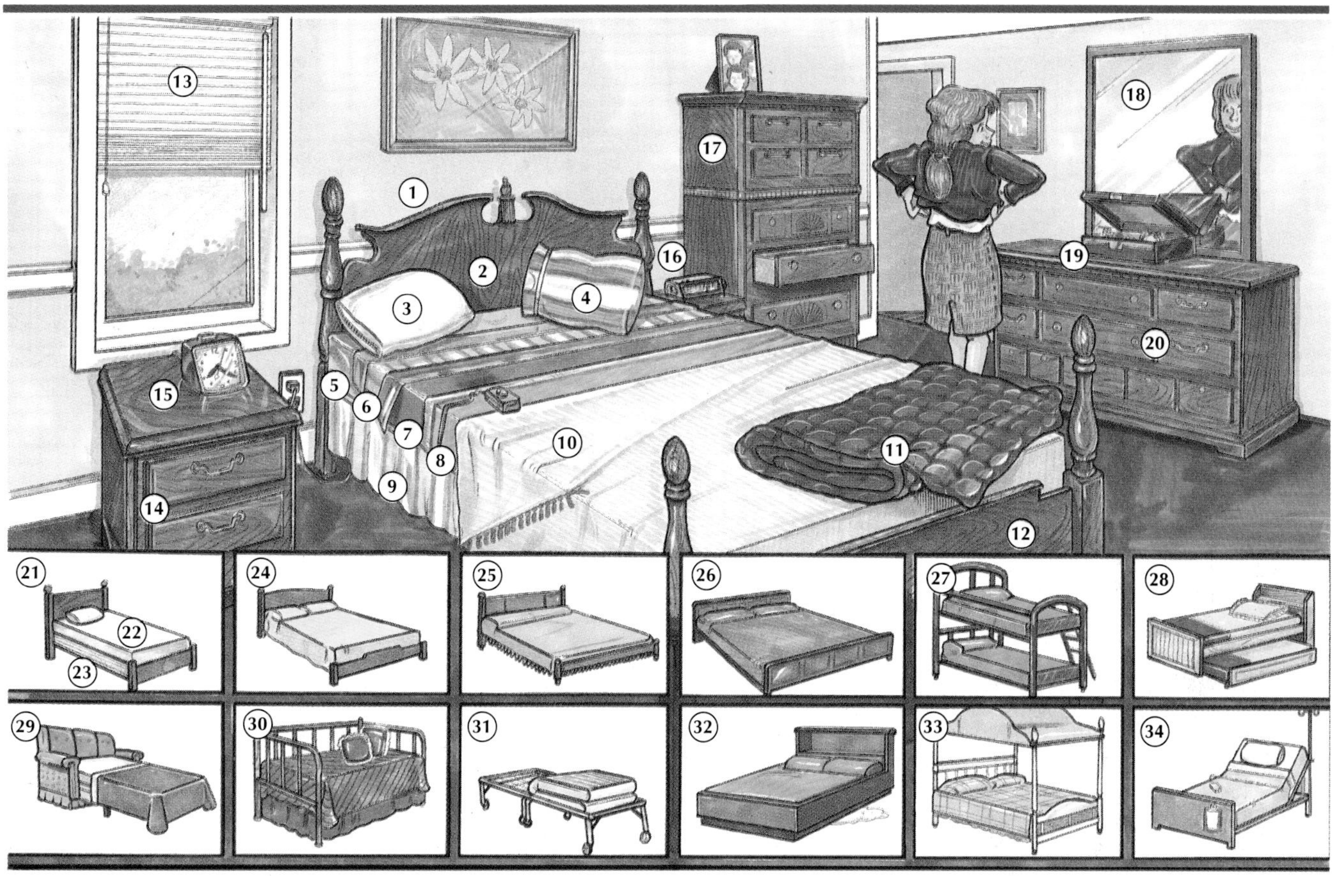

ベッド	**1.** bed
頭板	**2.** headboard
枕	**3.** pillow
枕カバー	**4.** pillowcase
シーツ	**5.** fitted sheet
上掛けシーツ	**6.** (flat) sheet
毛布	**7.** blanket
電気毛布	**8.** electric blanket
ひだ飾り	**9.** dust ruffle
ベッドカバー	**10.** bedspread
掛け布団	**11.** comforter/quilt
足板	**12.** footboard
ブラインド	**13.** blinds
サイドテーブル	**14.** night table/ nightstand
目覚まし時計	**15.** alarm clock
タイマー付ラジオ	**16.** clock radio
整理だんす	**17.** chest (of drawers)
鏡	**18.** mirror
宝石入れ	**19.** jewelry box
ドレッサー	**20.** dresser/bureau
ツインベッド（の片方）	**21.** twin bed
マットレス	**22.** mattress
寝台用スプリング	**23.** box spring
ダブルベッド	**24.** double bed
クイーンサイズベッド	**25.** queen-size bed
キングサイズベッド	**26.** king-size bed
2段ベッド	**27.** bunk bed
脚輪付きベッド	**28.** trundle bed
ソファベッド	**29.** sofa bed/ convertible sofa
寝台兼用の長いす	**30.** day bed
簡易ベッド	**31.** cot
ウォーターベッド	**32.** water bed
天蓋付ベッド	**33.** canopy bed
治療用ベッド	**34.** hospital bed

[In a store]

A. Excuse me. I'm looking for a/an ________.*
B. We have some very nice ________s. And they're all on sale this week.
A. Oh, good!

**With 13, use:* Excuse me. I'm looking for ________.

[In a bedroom]

A. Oh, no! I just lost my contact lens!
B. Where?
A. I think it's on the ________.
B. I'll help you look.

Tell about your bedroom.
(In my bedroom there's ....)

A. I think we need a new **dishwasher**.
B. I think you're right.

食器洗い機 **1.** dishwasher
食器洗い機用合成洗剤 **2.** dishwasher detergent
台所用洗剤 **3.** dishwashing liquid
蛇口 **4.** faucet
流し **5.** (kitchen) sink
ディスポーザー（ごみ処理機） **6.** (garbage) disposal
スポンジ **7.** sponge
みがきたわし **8.** scouring pad
なべ洗い **9.** pot scrubber
水切り **10.** dish rack
キッチンペーパーホルダー **11.** paper towel holder
ふきん **12.** dish towel
ごみ圧縮器 **13.** trash compactor
キャビネット（戸棚） **14.** cabinet
電子レンジ **15.** microwave (oven)
調理台 **16.** (kitchen) counter
まな板 **17.** cutting board
キャニスター（缶，箱） **18.** canister
レンジ **19.** stove/range
バーナー **20.** burner
オーブン（天火） **21.** oven
なべつかみ **22.** potholder
トースター **23.** toaster
調味料ラック **24.** spice rack
（電動）缶切り **25.** (electric) can opener
料理の本 **26.** cookbook
冷蔵庫 **27.** refrigerator
冷凍庫 **28.** freezer
製氷器 **29.** ice maker
製氷皿 **30.** ice tray
マグネット **31.** refrigerator magnet
テーブル **32.** kitchen table
ランチョンマット **33.** placemat
いす **34.** kitchen chair
ごみバケツ **35.** garbage pail

[In a store]
A. Excuse me. Are your ________s still on sale?
B. Yes, they are. They're twenty percent off.

[In a kitchen]
A. When did you get this/these new ________(s)?
B. I got it/them last week.

Tell about your kitchen.
(In my kitchen there's ....)

A. Could I possibly borrow your **wok**?
B. Sure. I'll get it for you right now.
A. Thanks.

中華なべ **1.** wok
深なべ **2.** pot
ミルクパン **3.** saucepan
ふた **4.** lid/cover/top
フライパン **5.** frying pan/skillet
あぶり皿 **6.** roasting pan
ロースター（焼きなべ） **7.** roaster
二重なべ **8.** double boiler
圧力なべ **9.** pressure cooker
水切り **10.** colander
キャセロール **11.** casserole (dish)
ケーキ型 **12.** cake pan
パイ皿 **13.** pie plate
クッキー用天パン **14.** cookie sheet
ボウル **15.** (mixing) bowl

めん棒 **16.** rolling pin
計量カップ **17.** measuring cup
計量スプーン **18.** measuring spoon
コーヒーメーカー **19.** coffeemaker
コーヒーひき **20.** coffee grinder
やかん **21.** tea kettle
オーブントースター **22.** toaster oven
電動泡立て器 **23.** (electric) mixer
フードプロセッサー **24.** food processor
電気グリル **25.** electric frying pan
ワッフル焼き型 **26.** waffle iron
鉄板/電気プレート **27.** (electric) griddle
ポップコーンメーカー **28.** popcorn maker
ミキサー **29.** blender

おろし器 **30.** grater
卵泡立て器 **31.** (egg) beater
玉じゃくし **32.** ladle
アイスクリームサーバー **33.** ice cream scoop
クッキー抜き型 **34.** cookie cutter
万能こし器 **35.** strainer
にんにくつぶし **36.** garlic press
せん抜き **37.** bottle opener
缶切り **38.** can opener
泡立て器 **39.** whisk
皮むき **40.** (vegetable) peeler
包丁 **41.** knife
フライ返し **42.** spatula
果物ナイフ **43.** paring knife

A. What are you looking for?
B. I'm looking for the ________.*
A. Did you look in the drawers/in the cabinets/next to the ________/...........?
B. Yes. I looked everywhere!

*With 2, 4, 12–15, 41, use:
I'm looking for a ________.

[A Commercial]

Come to *Kitchen World*! We have everything you need for your kitchen, from ________s and ________s, to ________s and ________s. Are you looking for a new ________? Is it time to throw out your old ________? Come to *Kitchen World* today! We have everything you need!

What things do you have in your kitchen?
Which things do you use very often?
Which things do you rarely use?

A. Thank you for the **teddy bear.** It's a very nice gift.
B. You're welcome. Tell me, when are you due?
A. In a few more weeks.

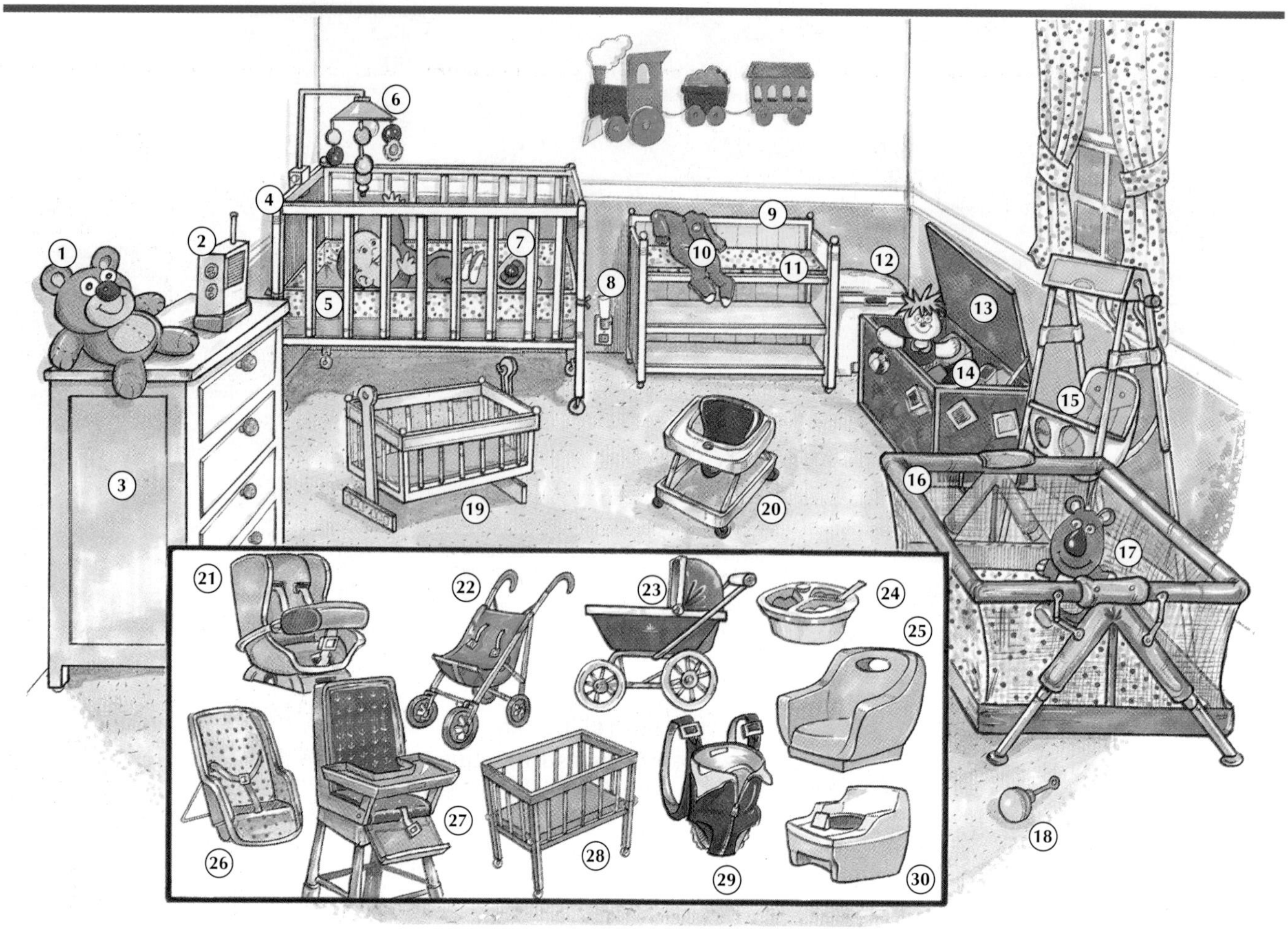

テディベア（熊のぬいぐるみ） **1.** teddy bear
インターホン **2.** intercom
整理だんす **3.** chest (of drawers)
ベビーベッド **4.** crib
ベッドの枠 **5.** crib bumper
ベッドメリー **6.** mobile
ベビートーイ **7.** crib toy
足元灯 **8.** night light
おむつ交換台 **9.** changing table/ dressing table
ロンパース（伸縮性のあるつなぎのベビー服） **10.** stretch suit

（おむつ交換用）マット **11.** changing pad
おむつバケツ **12.** diaper pail
おもちゃ箱 **13.** toy chest
人形 **14.** doll
ブランコ **15.** swing
プレイヤード **16.** playpen
ぬいぐるみ **17.** stuffed animal
ガラガラ **18.** rattle
ゆりかご **19.** cradle
歩行器 **20.** walker

チャイルドカーシート **21.** car seat
ベビーバギー **22.** stroller
大型ベビーカー **23.** baby carriage
フードウォーマ/保温器 **24.** food warmer
ブースターシート **25.** booster seat
ローチェア **26.** baby seat
ハイチェア **27.** high chair
（持ち運びできる）セカンドベッド **28.** portable crib
ベビーキャリア **29.** baby carrier
おまる **30.** potty

A. That's a very nice ________.
Where did you get it?
B. It was a gift from ....

A. Do you have everything you need before the baby comes?
B. Almost everything. We're still looking for a/an ________ and a/an ________.

Tell about your country:
What things do people buy for a new baby?
Does a new baby sleep in a separate room, as in the United States?

[1–12]
A. Do we need anything from the store?
B. Yes. Could you get some more **baby powder**?
A. Sure.

[13–17]
A. Do we need anything from the store?
B. Yes. Could you get another **pacifier**?
A. Sure.

ベビーパウダー	**1.** baby powder	おしり拭き	**7.** (baby) wipes	おしゃぶり	**13.** pacifier
ベビーローション	**2.** baby lotion	綿棒	**8.** cotton swabs	哺乳ビン	**14.** bottle
ベビーシャンプー	**3.** baby shampoo	おむつ止めピン	**9.** diaper pins	乳首	**15.** nipple
軟こう	**4.** ointment	紙おむつ	**10.** disposable diapers	よだれかけ	**16.** bib
乳児用人口乳（栄養食）	**5.** formula	布おむつ	**11.** cloth diapers	歯がため	**17.** teething ring
ベビーフード	**6.** baby food	ビタミン剤	**12.** (liquid) vitamins		

[In a store]
A. Excuse me. I can't find the ________.*
B. I'm sorry. We're out of ________.* We'll have some more tomorrow.

*With 13–17, use the plural.

[At home]
A. Honey? Where did you put the ________?
B. It's/They're in/on/next to the ________.

In your opinion, which are better: cloth diapers or disposable diapers? Why?

Tell about baby products in your country.

A. Where's the **plunger**?
B. It's *next to* the **toilet**.

A. Where's the **toothbrush**?
B. It's *in* the **toothbrush holder**.

A. Where's the **washcloth**?
B. It's *on* the **towel rack**.

A. Where's the **mirror**?
B. It's *over* the **sink**.

ブランジャー（排水管掃除棒）	**1.**	plunger
便器	**2.**	toilet
トイレタンク	**3.**	toilet tank
便座	**4.**	toilet seat
芳香剤	**5.**	air freshener
トイレットペーパーホルダー	**6.**	toilet paper holder
トイレットペーパー	**7.**	toilet paper
トイレブラシ	**8.**	toilet brush
タオル掛け	**9.**	towel rack
バスタオル	**10.**	bath towel
手ふきタオル	**11.**	hand towel
浴用タオル	**12.**	washcloth/ facecloth
洗濯かご	**13.**	hamper
体重計	**14.**	(bathroom) scale
棚	**15.**	shelf
ドライヤー	**16.**	hair dryer
換気扇	**17.**	fan
鏡	**18.**	mirror
薬用品棚	**19.**	medicine cabinet/ medicine chest
洗面台	**20.**	(bathroom) sink
湯栓	**21.**	hot water faucet
水栓	**22.**	cold water faucet
コップ	**23.**	cup
歯ブラシ	**24.**	toothbrush
歯ブラシ立て	**25.**	toothbrush holder
石けん	**26.**	soap
石けん受け	**27.**	soap dish
石けん入れ	**28.**	soap dispenser
ウォーター・ピック（商標名：歯の洗浄器）	**29.**	Water Pik
化粧台	**30.**	vanity
くずかご	**31.**	wastebasket
シャワー	**32.**	shower
シャワーカーテンレール	**33.**	shower curtain rod
シャワーヘッド	**34.**	shower head
カーテンリング	**35.**	shower curtain rings
シャワーカーテン	**36.**	shower curtain
浴槽	**37.**	bathtub/tub
排水溝	**38.**	drain
浴槽敷き	**39.**	rubber mat
スポンジ	**40.**	sponge
バスマット	**41.**	bath mat/bath rug

A. [Knock. Knock.] Did I leave my glasses in there?
B. Yes. They're on/in/next to the ________.

A. *Bobby?*
B. Yes, Mom/Dad?
A. You didn't clean up the bathroom! There's toothpaste on the ________ and there's powder all over the ________!
B. Sorry, Mom/Dad. I'll clean it up right away.

Tell about your bathroom.
(In my bathroom there's ....)

[1–17]
A. Excuse me. Where can I find **toothbrush**es?
B. They're in the next aisle.
A. Thank you.

[18–38]
A. Excuse me. Where can I find **shampoo**?
B. It's in the next aisle.
A. Thank you.

歯ブラシ **1.** toothbrush
くし **2.** comb
ブラシ **3.** (hair) brush
カミソリ **4.** razor
カミソリの刃 **5.** razor blades
電気カミソリ **6.** electric razor/ electric shaver
止血棒剤(ひげそり傷の止血用) **7.** styptic pencil
シャワーキャップ **8.** shower cap
つめやすり **9.** nail file
(マニキュア用の) つめやすり **10.** emery board
つめ切り **11.** nail clipper
(マニキュア用) つめブラシ **12.** nail brush
はさみ **13.** scissors
毛抜き **14.** tweezers
ボビーピン **15.** bobby pins
ヘアピン **16.** hair clips
髪止め飾りピン **17.** barrettes
シャンプー **18.** shampoo
リンス **19.** conditioner/rinse
ヘアスプレー **20.** hairspray
歯みがき粉 **21.** toothpaste
うがい薬 **22.** mouthwash
デンタルフロス **23.** dental floss
ひげそり用クリーム **24.** shaving creme
アフターシェーブローション **25.** after shave lotion
脱臭剤 **26.** deodorant
パウダー (粉おしろい) **27.** powder
ハンドローション **28.** hand lotion
香水 **29.** perfume/cologne
靴みがき **30.** shoe polish
マニキュア液 **31.** nail polish
除光液 **32.** nail polish remover

化粧 **makeup**
ファウンデーション **33.** base/foundation
ほお紅 **34.** blush/rouge
口紅 **35.** lipstick
アイシャドー **36.** eye shadow
アイライナー **37.** eye liner
マスカラ **38.** mascara

A. I'm going to the drug store to get a/an ________.*
B. While you're there, could you also get a/an ________?*
A. Sure.

**With 5, 13–38, use: get ________.*

A. Do you have everything for the trip?
B. I think so.
A. Did you remember to pack your ________?
B. Oops! I forgot. Thanks for reminding me.

You're going on a trip. Make a list of personal care products you need to take with you.

HOUSEHOLD CLEANING AND LAUNDRY［家庭の掃除・洗濯用品］

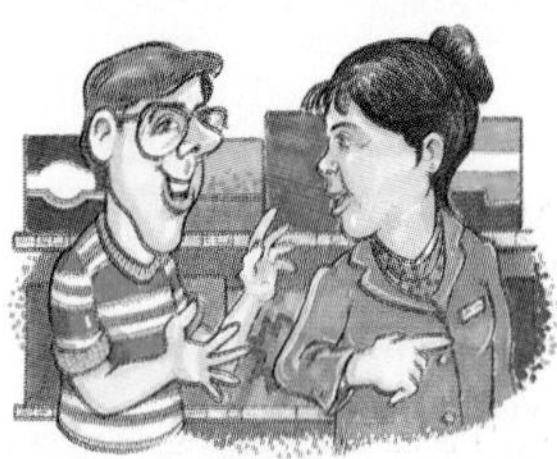

[1–17, 28–39]
A. Excuse me. Do you sell **broom**s?
B. Yes. They're at the back of the store.
A. Thanks.

[18–27]
A. Excuse me. Do you sell **laundry detergent**?
B. Yes. It's at the back of the store.
A. Thanks.

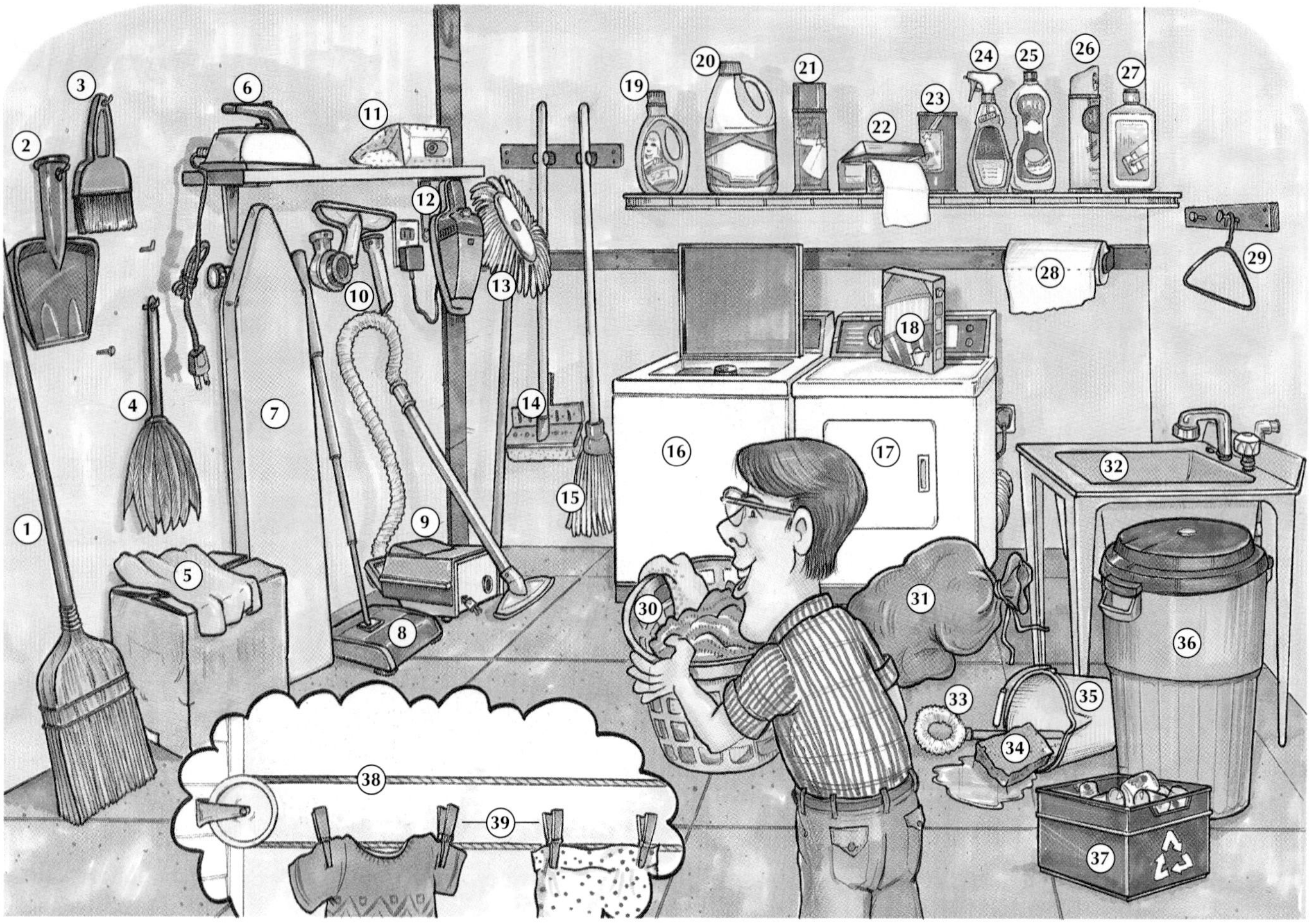

ほうき **1.** broom
ちりとり **2.** dustpan
小ぼうき **3.** whisk broom
はたき **4.** feather duster
ぞうきん **5.** dust cloth
アイロン **6.** iron
アイロン台 **7.** ironing board
じゅうたん掃除機 **8.** carpet sweeper
掃除機 **9.** vacuum (cleaner)
掃除機付属品 **10.** vacuum cleaner attachments
掃除機用ゴミバッグ **11.** vacuum cleaner bag
ハンドクリーナー **12.** hand vacuum
ダストモップ **13.** (dust) mop/(dry) mop
スポンジモップ **14.** (sponge) mop
モップ **15.** (wet) mop
洗濯機 **16.** washing machine/washer
乾燥機 **17.** dryer
洗濯用合成洗剤 **18.** laundry detergent
柔軟剤 **19.** fabric softener
漂白剤 **20.** bleach
洗濯のり **21.** starch
静電気とり **22.** static cling remover
クレンザー **23.** cleanser
窓用洗剤 **24.** window cleaner
アンモニア **25.** ammonia
家具用洗剤/家具みがき **26.** furniture polish
ワックス **27.** floor wax
ペーパータオル **28.** paper towels
ハンガー **29.** hanger
洗濯かご **30.** laundry basket
洗濯物袋 **31.** laundry bag
流し **32.** utility sink
たわし **33.** scrub brush
スポンジ **34.** sponge
バケツ **35.** bucket/pail
ごみバケツ **36.** trash can/garbage can
リサイクル用品入れ **37.** recycling bin
物干しひも **38.** clothesline
洗濯ばさみ **39.** clothespins

A. How do you like this/these ______?
B. It's/They're great!

A. They're having a big sale at Dave's Discount Store this week.
B. Oh, really? What's on sale?
A. [18–27] and [1–17, 28–39] s.

Who does the cleaning and laundry in your home? What things does that person use?

A. When are you going to repair the **lamppost**?
B. I'm going to repair it next Saturday.

街燈柱	**1.** lamppost	雨戸	**12.** shutter	裏口	**22.** back door
郵便ポスト	**2.** mailbox	屋根	**13.** roof	ドアの取っ手	**23.** doorknob
玄関口	**3.** front walk	テレビアンテナ	**14.** TV antenna	網戸	**24.** screen door
玄関口の階段	**4.** front steps	煙突	**15.** chimney	勝手口	**25.** side door
ポーチ	**5.** (front) porch	車庫	**16.** garage	衛星放送アンテナ	**26.** satellite dish
風よけドア	**6.** storm door	車庫入り口	**17.** garage door	テラス	**27.** patio
玄関ドア	**7.** front door	ドライブウェイ（私設車道）	**18.** driveway	芝刈り機	**28.** lawnmower
呼び鈴	**8.** doorbell	雨どい	**19.** gutter	バーベキューグリル	**29.** barbecue/ (outdoor)grill
照明/玄関灯	**9.** (front) light	縦どい	**20.** drainpipe/ downspout	庭いす	**30.** lawn chair
窓	**10.** window	ベランダ/デッキ	**21.** deck	物置	**31.** tool shed
網戸	**11.** (window) screen				

[On the telephone]
A. Harry's Home Repairs.
B. Hello. Do you fix ________s?
A. No, we don't.
B. Oh, okay. Thank you.

[At work on Monday morning]
A. What did you do this weekend?
B. Nothing much. I repaired my ________ and my ________.

Do you like to repair things?
What things can you repair yourself?
What things can't you repair? Who repairs them?

A. Is there a **lobby**?
B. Yes, there is. Do you want to see the apartment?
A. Yes, I do.

玄関ホール	**1.** lobby	のぞき穴	**8.** peephole	管理人	**15.** superintendent
インターホン	**2.** intercom	ドアチェーン	**9.** (door) chain	倉庫	**16.** storage room
ブザー	**3.** buzzer	本締錠	**10.** dead-bolt lock	パーキングビル	**17.** parking garage
郵便受け	**4.** mailbox	エアコン（空調設備）	**11.** air conditioner	駐車場	**18.** parking lot
エレベーター	**5.** elevator	火災報知器	**12.** fire alarm	バルコニー	**19.** balcony/terrace
ドアマン（玄関番）	**6.** doorman	ダストシュート	**13.** garbage chute	プール	**20.** swimming pool
煙感知器	**7.** smoke detector	洗濯室	**14.** laundry room	ワールプール/ジャクージー	**21.** whirlpool

[Renting an apartment]

A. Let me show you around the building.*
B. Okay.
A. This is the ________ and here's the ________.
B. I see.

**With 7–11, use:*
Let me show you around the apartment.

[On the telephone]

A. Mom and Dad? I found an apartment.
B. Good. Tell us about it.
A. It has a/an ________ and a/an ________.
B. That's nice. Does it have a/an ________?
A. Yes, it does.

Tell about the differences between living in a house and in an apartment building.

A. Did you remember to pay the **carpenter**?
B. Yes. I wrote a check yesterday.

- 大工 **1.** carpenter
- 便利屋 **2.** handyman
- ペンキ屋 **3.** (house) painter
- 煙突掃除夫 **4.** chimney sweep
- 家庭電気器具修理屋 **5.** appliance repair person
- テレビ修理屋 **6.** TV repair person
- 錠前師 **7.** locksmith
- 庭師 **8.** gardener
- 電気工 **9.** electrician
- 配管工 **10.** plumber
- 害虫駆除業者 **11.** exterminator
- ガス料金請求書 **12.** gas bill
- 電気料金請求書 **13.** electric bill
- 電話料金請求書 **14.** telephone bill
- 水道料金請求書 **15.** water bill
- 燃料費請求書 **16.** oil bill/ heating bill
- ケーブルテレビ料金請求書 **17.** cable TV bill
- 害虫予防費請求書 **18.** pest control bill
- 家賃 **19.** rent
- 駐車料金 **20.** parking fee
- 住宅ローン返済金 **21.** mortgage payment

[1–11]
A. When is the ________ going to come?
B. This afternoon.

[12–21]
A. When is the ________ due?
B. It's due at the end of the month.

Tell about utilities, services, and repairs you pay for. How much do you pay?

A. Could I borrow your **hammer***?
B. Sure.
A. Thanks.

**With 28–32, use:* Could I borrow some ________s?

金づち **1.** hammer
ドライバー/ねじ回し **2.** screwdriver
十字ドライバー **3.** Phillips screwdriver
スパナ **4.** wrench
ペンチ **5.** pliers
金のこ **6.** hacksaw
手おの **7.** hatchet
モンキーレンチ **8.** monkey wrench
のこぎり **9.** saw
手回しドリル **10.** hand drill
（ドリルの）曲がり柄 **11.** brace

のみ **12.** chisel
はぎとり器 **13.** scraper
万力 **14.** vise
電気ドリル **15.** electric drill
ドリルの刃 **16.** (drill) bit
動力のこぎり **17.** power saw
水準器 **18.** level
かんな **19.** plane
道具箱 **20.** toolbox
ペンキ皿 **21.** (paint) pan
ペンキローラー **22.** (paint) roller

ペンキはけ **23.** paintbrush/brush
ペンキ **24.** paint
シンナー **25.** paint thinner
紙やすり **26.** sandpaper
針金 **27.** wire
くぎ **28.** nail
ねじ **29.** screw
ワッシャー **30.** washer
ボルト **31.** bolt
ナット **32.** nut

[1–4, 6–27]
A. Where's the ________?
B. It's on/next to/near/over/under the ________.

[5, 28–32]
A. Where are the ________(s)?
B. They're on/next to/near/over/under the ________.

Do you like to work with tools?
What tools do you have in your home?

[1–16]
A. I can't find the **lawnmower**!
B. Look in the tool shed.
A. I did.
B. Oh! Wait a minute! I lent the **lawnmower** to the neighbors.

[17–32]
A. I can't find the **flashlight**!
B. Look in the utility cabinet.
A. I did.
B. Oh! Wait a minute! I lent the **flashlight** to the neighbors.

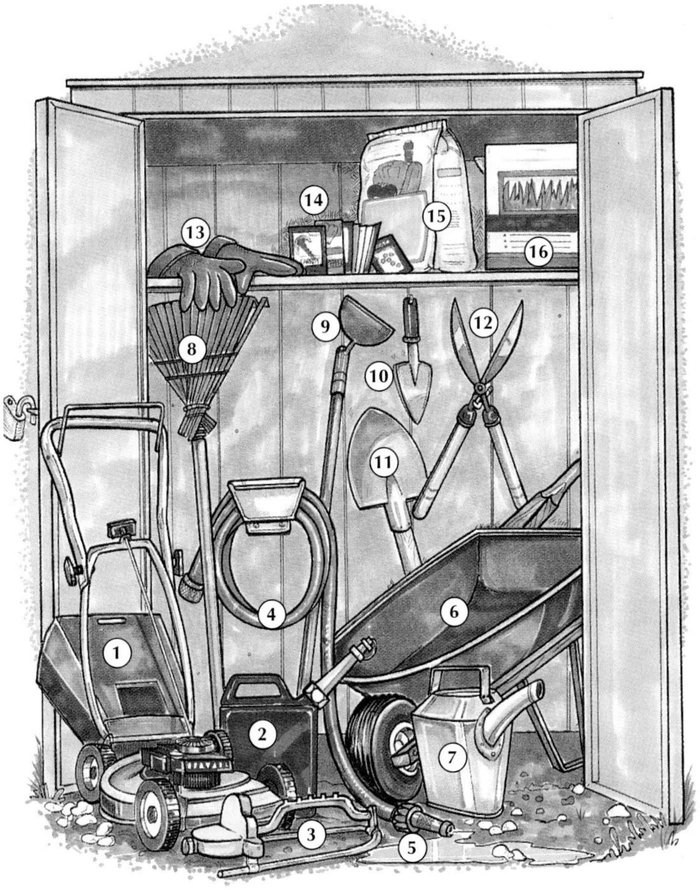

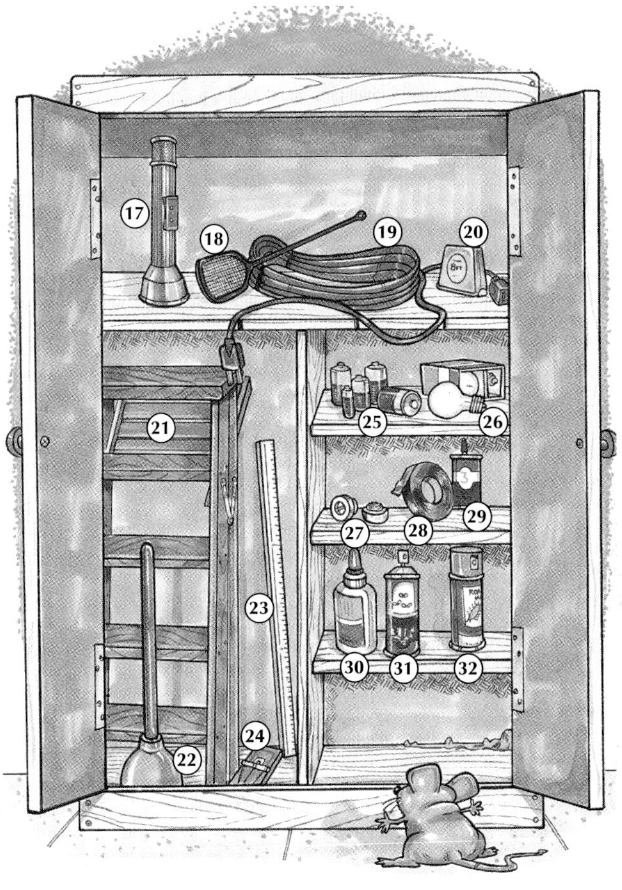

芝刈り機 **1.** lawnmower
ガソリン入れ **2.** gas can
スプリンクラー **3.** sprinkler
ホース **4.** (garden) hose
ノズル **5.** nozzle
手押し車 **6.** wheelbarrow
じょうろ **7.** watering can
くま手 **8.** rake
くわ **9.** hoe
移植ごて **10.** trowel
シャベル **11.** shovel
刈り込みばさみ **12.** hedge clippers
軍手/作業手袋 **13.** work gloves
野菜の種 **14.** vegetable seeds
肥料 **15.** fertilizer
芝の種 **16.** grass seed
懐中電灯 **17.** flashlight
ハエたたき **18.** fly swatter
延長コード **19.** extension cord
巻き尺 **20.** tape measure
脚立 **21.** step ladder
プランジャー/吸引式下水掃除棒 **22.** plunger
ヤード尺 **23.** yardstick
ねずみ取り **24.** mousetrap
電池 **25.** batteries
電球 **26.** lightbulbs/bulbs
ヒューズ **27.** fuses
絶縁テープ **28.** electrical tape
機械油 **29.** oil
接着剤 **30.** glue
殺虫剤 **31.** bug spray/insect spray
ゴキブリ用殺虫剤 **32.** roach killer

[1–11, 17–24]
A. I'm going to the hardware store. Can you think of anything we need?
B. Yes. We need a/an ________.
A. Oh, that's right.

[12–16, 25–32]
A. I'm going to the hardware store. Can you think of anything we need?
B. Yes. We need ________.
A. Oh, that's right.

What gardening tools and home supplies do you have? Tell about how and when you use each one.

基数/Cardinal Numbers

1	one	11	eleven	21	twenty-one	101	one hundred (and) one
2	two	12	twelve	22	twenty-two	102	one hundred (and) two
3	three	13	thirteen	30	thirty	1,000	one thousand
4	four	14	fourteen	40	forty	10,000	ten thousand
5	five	15	fifteen	50	fifty	100,000	one hundred thousand
6	six	16	sixteen	60	sixty	1,000,000	one million
7	seven	17	seventeen	70	seventy		
8	eight	18	eighteen	80	eighty		
9	nine	19	nineteen	90	ninety		
10	ten	20	twenty	100	one hundred		

A. How old are you?
B. I'm ________ years old.

A. How many people are there in your family?
B. ________.

序数/Ordinal Numbers （第～の）

1st	first	11th	eleventh	21st	twenty-first	101st	one hundred (and) first
2nd	second	12th	twelfth	22nd	twenty-second	102nd	one hundred (and) second
3rd	third	13th	thirteenth	30th	thirtieth	1000th	one thousandth
4th	fourth	14th	fourteenth	40th	fortieth	10,000th	ten thousandth
5th	fifth	15th	fifteenth	50th	fiftieth	100,000th	one hundred thousandth
6th	sixth	16th	sixteenth	60th	sixtieth	1,000,000th	one millionth
7th	seventh	17th	seventeenth	70th	seventieth		
8th	eighth	18th	eighteenth	80th	eightieth		
9th	ninth	19th	nineteenth	90th	ninetieth		
10th	tenth	20th	twentieth	100th	one hundredth		

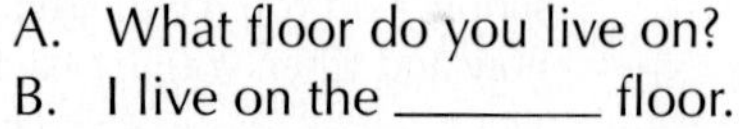

A. What floor do you live on?
B. I live on the ________ floor.

A. Is this the first time you've seen this movie?
B. No. It's the ________ time.

算数/Arithmetic

たし算 addition
2 **plus** 1 **equals*** 3.
2たす1は3。

ひき算 subtraction
8 **minus** 3 **equals*** 5.
8ひく3は5。

かけ算 multiplication
4 **times** 2 **equals*** 8.
4かける2は8。

わり算 division
10 **divided by** 2 **equals*** 5.
10わる2は5。

*isでも同じです。 *You can also say: **is**

A. How much is *two plus one*?
B. *Two plus one* equals/is *three*.

Make conversations for the arithmetic problems above and others.

分数/Fractions

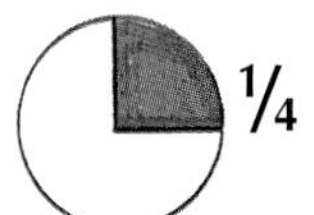

one quarter/ one fourth
4分の1

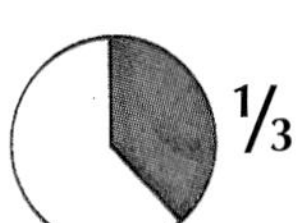

one third
3分の1

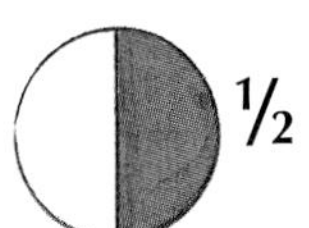

one half/half
2分の1

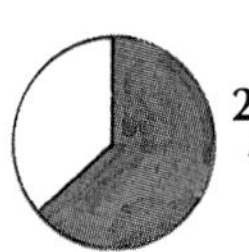

two thirds
3分の2

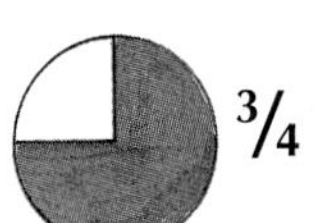

three quarters/ three fourths
4分の3

A. Is this on sale?
B. Yes. It's ________ off the regular price.

A. Is the gas tank almost empty?
B. It's about ________ full.

パーセント/Percents

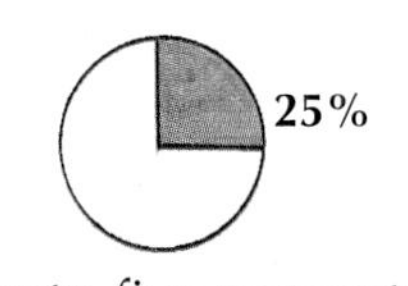

twenty-five percent
25パーセント

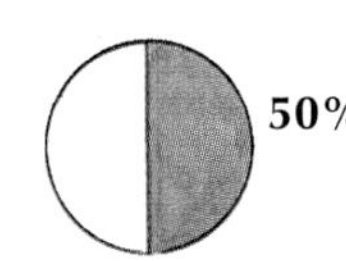

fifty percent
50パーセント

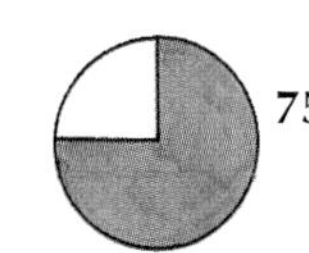

seventy-five percent
75パーセント

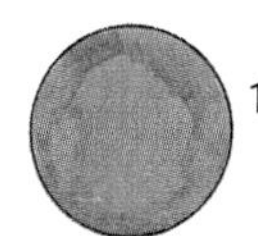

one hundred percent
100パーセント

A. How did you do on the test?
B. I got ________ percent of the answers right.

A. What's the weather forecast?
B. There's a ________ percent chance of rain.

Research and discuss:
What percentage of the people in your country live in cities? live on farms? work in factories? vote in national elections?

2:00

two o'clock
2時

2:15

two fifteen/
a quarter after *two*
2時15分

2:30

two thirty/
half past *two*
2時半

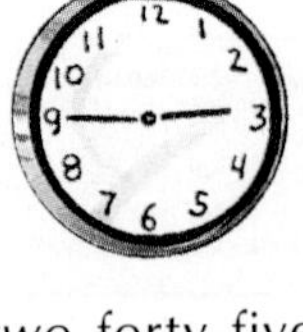
2:45

two forty-five/
a quarter to *three*
2時45分

2:05

two oh five
2時5分

2:20

two twenty/
twenty after *two*
2時20分

2:40

two forty/
twenty to *three*
2時40分

2:55

two fifty-five/
five to *three*

2時55分

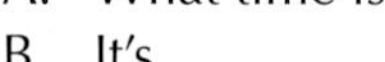

A. What time is it?
B. It's ________.

A. What time does the movie begin?
B. At ________.

two a.m.
午前2時

two p.m.
午後2時

noon/twelve noon
正午

midnight/
twelve midnight
午前0時

A. When does the train leave?
B. At ________.

A. What time will we arrive?
B. At ________.

Tell about your daily schedule:
What do you do? When?
(I get up at ________. I ....)
Do you usually have enough time to do things, or do you run out of time? Explain.
If there were 25 hours in a day, what would you do with the extra hour? Why?

Tell about the use of time in different cultures or countries you are familiar with:
Do people arrive on time for work? appointments? parties?
Do trains and buses operate exactly on schedule?
Do movies and sports events begin on time?
Do workplaces use time clocks or timesheets to record employees' work hours?

1999 **JANUARY** 1999

SUN	MON	TUE	WED	THUR	FRI	SAT
					1	2
3	4	5	6	7	8	9
10	11	12	13	14	15	16
17	18	19	20	21	22	23
24/31	25	26	27	28	29	30

年 **1. year**

1999年 nineteen ninety-nine

月 **2. month**

1月 January
2月 February
3月 March
4月 April
5月 May
6月 June
7月 July
8月 August
9月 September
10月 October
11月 November
12月 December

曜日 **3. day**

日曜日 Sunday
月曜日 Monday
火曜日 Tuesday
水曜日 Wednesday
木曜日 Thursday
金曜日 Friday
土曜日 Saturday

日付 **4. date**

1999年1月2日 January 2, 1999
1/2/99
January second,
nineteen ninety-nine

A. What year is it?
B. It's ________.

A. What month is it?
B. It's ________.

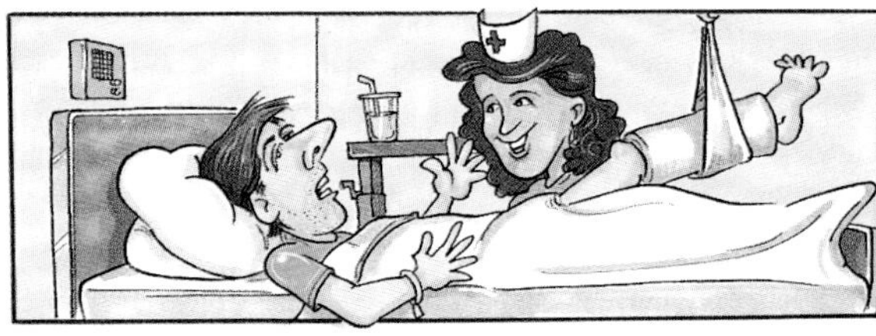

A. What day is it?
B. It's ________.

A. What's today's date?
B. Today is ________.

When did you begin to study English?
What days of the week do you study English? (I study English on ________.)

When is your birthday? (My birthday is on ________.)
What are your favorite months of the year? Why?
What are your least favorite months of the year? Why?

A. Where are you going?
B. I'm going to the **appliance store**.

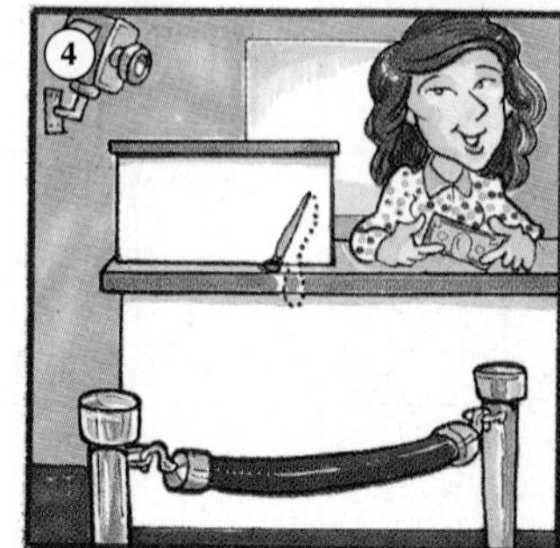

電気屋 **1.** appliance store
自動車販売店 **2.** auto dealer/ car dealer
パン屋 **3.** bakery
銀行 **4.** bank
床屋 **5.** barber shop

本屋 **6.** book store
バス発着所 **7.** bus station
カフェテリア **8.** cafeteria
託児所 **9.** child-care center/ day-care center
クリーニング店 **10.** cleaners/dry cleaners

ドーナツ店 **11.** donut shop
診療所 **12.** clinic
衣料品店 **13.** clothing store
喫茶店 **14.** coffee shop
コンピューター販売店/OA店 **15.** computer store

16

17

18

19

20

21

22

23

24

25

26

27

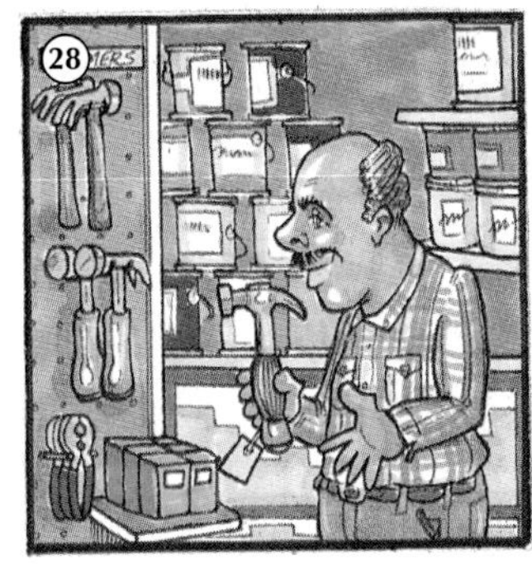
28

29

30

コンサートホール **16.** concert hall
コンビニエンスストア **17.** convenience store
コピーセンター **18.** copy center
デリカテッセン/総菜屋 **19.** delicatessen/deli
デパート **20.** department store
ディスカウントショップ **21.** discount store

薬局 **22.** drug store/ pharmacy
花屋 **23.** flower shop/florist
家具店 **24.** furniture store
ガソリンスタンド **25.** gas station/ service station

食料雑貨店 **26.** grocery store
美容院 **27.** hair salon
金物屋 **28.** hardware store
スポーツクラブ/ヘルスクラブ **29.** health club/spa
病院 **30.** hospital

A. Hi! How are you today?
B. Fine. Where are you going?
A. To the ________. How about you?
B. I'm going to the ________.

A. Oh, no! I can't find my wallet/purse!
B. Did you leave it at the ________?
A. Maybe I did.

Which of these places are in your neighborhood?
(In my neighborhood there's a/an …………)

A. Where's the **hotel**?
B. It's right over there.

ホテル **1.** hotel
アイスクリーム店 **2.** ice cream shop
宝石店 **3.** jewelry store
コインランドリー **4.** laundromat
図書館 **5.** library
マタニティー用品店 **6.** maternity shop
モーテル **7.** motel
映画館 **8.** movie theater
美術館 **9.** museum
レコード・CD店 **10.** music store
ナイトクラブ **11.** night club
公園 **12.** park
パーキングビル **13.** (parking) garage
駐車場 **14.** parking lot
ペットショップ **15.** pet shop

写真屋 **16.** photo shop
ピザ屋 **17.** pizza shop
郵便局 **18.** post office
レストラン **19.** restaurant
学校 **20.** school

靴屋 **21.** shoe store
ショッピングモール **22.** (shopping) mall
スーパーマーケット **23.** supermarket
劇場 **24.** theater
おもちゃ屋 **25.** toy store

駅 **26.** train station
旅行代理店 **27.** travel agency
ビデオショップ **28.** video store
めがね屋 **29.** vision center/ eyeglass store
動物園 **30.** zoo

A. Is there a/an ________ nearby?
B. Yes. There's a/an ________ around the corner.

A. Excuse me. Where's the ________?
B. It's down the street, next to the ________.
A. Thank you.

Which of these places are in your neighborhood?
(In my neighborhood there's a/an ....)

A. Where's the ________?
B. On/In/Next to/Between/Across from/ In front of/Behind/Under/Over the ________.

くず入れ **1.** trash container
警察署 **2.** police station
拘置所 **3.** jail
裁判所 **4.** courthouse
ベンチ **5.** bench
街灯 **6.** street light
アイスクリーム販売車 **7.** ice cream truck
歩道 **8.** sidewalk
縁石 **9.** curb
車道/通り **10.** street
マンホール **11.** manhole
バス停 **12.** bus stop
タクシー **13.** taxi/cab/taxicab
タクシー運転手 **14.** taxi driver/cab driver
バス **15.** bus
バス運転手 **16.** bus driver
パーキングメーター **17.** parking meter
（駐車違反を取り締まる）婦人警官 **18.** meter maid
地下鉄 **19.** subway
地下鉄の駅 **20.** subway station

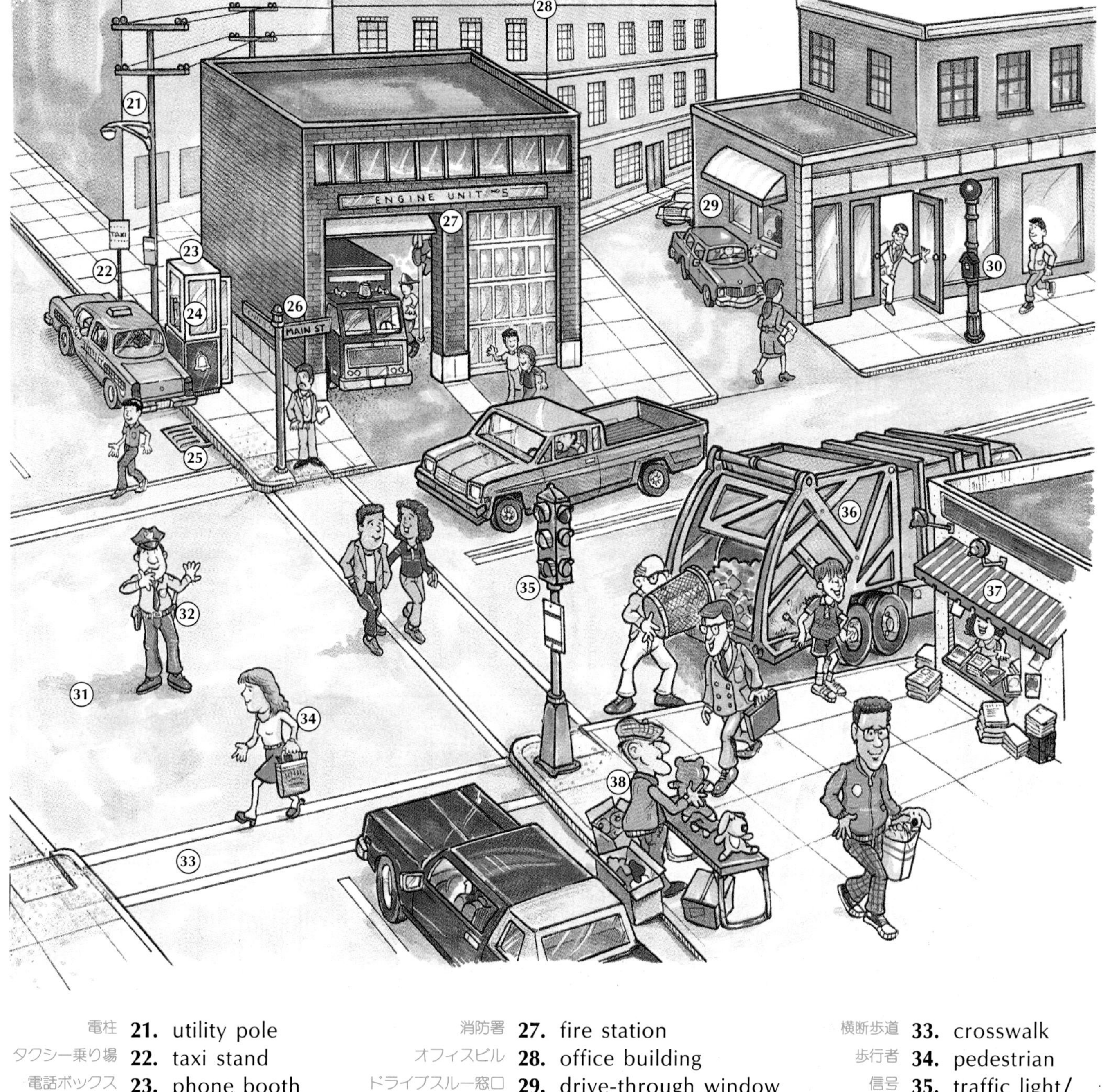

電柱	**21.** utility pole	消防署	**27.** fire station	横断歩道	**33.** crosswalk
タクシー乗り場	**22.** taxi stand	オフィスビル	**28.** office building	歩行者	**34.** pedestrian
電話ボックス	**23.** phone booth	ドライブスルー窓口	**29.** drive-through window	信号	**35.** traffic light/ traffic signal
公衆電話	**24.** public telephone	火災報知器	**30.** fire alarm box	清掃車	**36.** garbage truck
下水道	**25.** sewer	交差点	**31.** intersection	新聞スタンド	**37.** newsstand
街路標識	**26.** street sign	警官	**32.** police officer	露店商	**38.** street vendor

[An Election Speech]

If I am elected mayor, I'll take care of all the problems we have in our city. We need to do something about our ________s. We also need to do something about our ________s. And look at our ________s! We REALLY need to do something about THEM! We need a new mayor who can solve these problems. If I am elected mayor, we'll be proud of our ________s, ________s, and ________s again! Vote for me!

Step outside. Look around. Describe everything you see.

(背が) 高い−低い	**1– 2**	tall-short
(髪が) 長い−短い	**3– 4**	long-short
(からだが) 大きい−小さい	**5– 6**	large/big-small/little
(高さが) 高い−低い	**7– 8**	high-low
太っている−やせている	**9–10**	heavy/fat-thin/skinny
重い−軽い	**11–12**	heavy-light
(服が) ゆるい−きつい	**13–14**	loose-tight
(速さが) 速い−おそい	**15–16**	fast-slow
(道が) まっすぐな−曲がった	**17–18**	straight-crooked
(髪が) まっすぐな−巻き毛の	**19–20**	straight-curly
(幅が) 広い−狭い	**21–22**	wide-narrow
太い/厚い−細い/薄い	**23–24**	thick-thin
暗い−明るい	**25–26**	dark-light
新しい−古い	**27–28**	new-old
若い−年とった	**29–30**	young-old
(仲が) よい−わるい	**31–32**	good-bad
熱い−冷たい	**33–34**	hot-cold
やわらかい−かたい	**35–36**	soft-hard
かんたんな−むずかしい	**37–38**	easy-difficult/hard
(肌が) なめらかな−ざらざらの	**39–40**	smooth-rough
かたづいた−散らかった	**41–42**	neat-messy
きれいな−よごれた	**43–44**	clean-dirty
そうぞうしい−静かな	**45–46**	noisy/loud-quiet
結婚している−独身の	**47–48**	married-single
裕福な−貧しい	**49–50**	rich/wealthy-poor

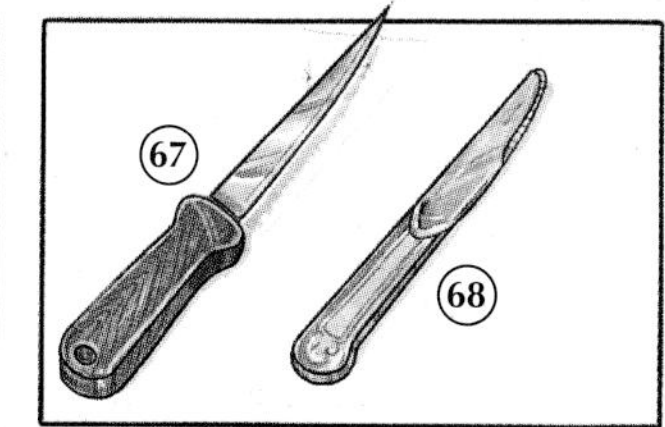

美しい一醜い **51–52** pretty/beautiful-ugly
ハンサムな一醜い **53–54** handsome-ugly
ぬれた一乾いた **55–56** wet-dry
開いている一閉じている **57–58** open-closed
いっぱいの一からの **59–60** full-empty
（値段が）高い一安い/高くない **61–62** expensive-cheap/inexpensive
（服が）はでな一じみな **63–64** fancy-plain
つやのある一くすんだ **65–66** shiny-dull
（刃の先が）とがった一とがっていない **67–68** sharp-dull

[1–2]
A. Is your sister **tall**?
B. No. She's **short**.

1–2 Is your sister ________?
3–4 Is his hair ________?
5–6 Is their dog ________?
7–8 Is the bridge ________?
9–10 Is your friend ________?
11–12 Is the box ________?
13–14 Are the pants ________?
15–16 Is the train ________?
17–18 Is the path ________?
19–20 Is his hair ________?
21–22 Is that street ________?
23–24 Is the line ________?
25–26 Is the room ________?
27–28 Is your car ________?
29–30 Is he ________?
31–32 Are your neighbor's children ________?
33–34 Is the water ________?
35–36 Is your pillow ________?
37–38 Is today's homework ________?
39–40 Is your skin ________?
41–42 Is your desk ________?
43–44 Are the dishes ________?
45–46 Is your neighbor ________?
47–48 Is your sister ________?
49–50 Is your uncle ________?
51–52 Is the witch ________?
53–54 Is the pirate ________?
55–56 Are the clothes ________?
57–58 Is the door ________?
59–60 Is the pitcher ________?
61–62 Is that restaurant ________?
63–64 Is the dress ________?
65–66 Is your kitchen floor ________?
67–68 Is the knife ________?

A. Tell me about your ....
B. He's/She's/It's/They're ________.

A. Is your .... ________?
B. No, not at all. As a matter of fact, he's/she's/it's/they're ________.

Describe yourself.
Describe a person you know.
Describe one of your favorite places.

A. You look **tired**.
B. I am. I'm VERY **tired**.

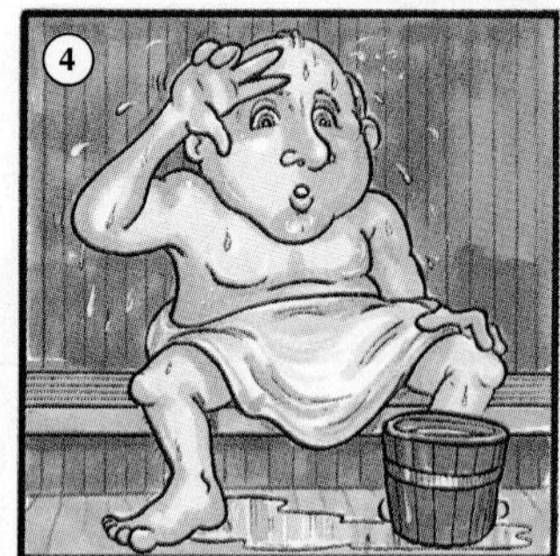

疲れた **1.** tired
眠い **2.** sleepy
疲れきった **3.** exhausted
暑い **4.** hot
寒い **5.** cold
おなかがすいた **6.** hungry

のどがかわいた **7.** thirsty
おなかがいっぱいの **8.** full
気分がわるい **9.** sick/ill
楽しい **10.** happy
有頂天の **11.** ecstatic

悲しい **12.** sad/unhappy
みじめな **13.** miserable
うれしい **14.** pleased
がっかりした **15.** disappointed
うろたえた **16.** upset

いらいらした **17.** annoyed
失敗した/くじかれた **18.** frustrated
怒った **19.** angry/mad
激怒した **20.** furious
うんざりした **21.** disgusted
びっくりした **22.** surprised

ショックを受けた **23.** shocked
落ち着かない **24.** nervous
心配した **25.** worried
こわがった **26.** scared/afraid
あきた **27.** bored

誇りに思った **28.** proud
どぎまぎした **29.** embarrassed
恥じた **30.** ashamed
うらやましい **31.** jealous
頭が混乱した/途方にくれた **32.** confused

A. Are you ________?
B. No. Why do you ask? Do I LOOK ________?
A. Yes. You do.

A. I'm ________.
B. Why?
A. ....

What makes you happy? sad? mad?
When do you feel nervous? annoyed?
Do you ever feel embarrassed? When?

[1–22]
A. This **apple** is delicious! Where did you get it?
B. At *Shaw's Supermarket.*

[23–31]
A. These **grapes** are delicious! Where did you get them?
B. At *Farmer Fred's Fruit Stand.*

リンゴ	**1.**	apple
桃	**2.**	peach
西洋ナシ	**3.**	pear
バナナ	**4.**	banana
スモモ/プラム	**5.**	plum
アンズ	**6.**	apricot
ネクタリン	**7.**	nectarine
キウイ	**8.**	kiwi
パパイヤ	**9.**	papaya
マンゴー	**10.**	mango
イチジク	**11.**	fig
ココナツ	**12.**	coconut
アボカド	**13.**	avocado
カンタループメロン	**14.**	cantaloupe
ハネーデューメロン	**15.**	honeydew (melon)
パイナップル	**16.**	pineapple
スイカ	**17.**	watermelon
グレープフルーツ	**18.**	grapefruit
レモン	**19.**	lemon
ライム	**20.**	lime
オレンジ	**21.**	orange
タンジェリン	**22.**	tangerine
ブドウ	**23.**	grapes
サクランボ	**24.**	cherries
プルーン	**25.**	prunes
ナツメヤシ	**26.**	dates
干しブドウ	**27.**	raisins
ブルーベリー	**28.**	blueberries
ツルコケモモ/クランベリー	**29.**	cranberries
木イチゴ/ラズベリー	**30.**	raspberries
イチゴ	**31.**	strawberries

A. I'm hungry. Do we have any fruit?
B. Yes. We have ________s* and ________s.*

**With 14–18, use:*
We have _______ and _______.

A. Do we have any more ________s?†
B. No. I'll get some more when I go to the supermarket.

†With 14–18, use:
Do we have any more _______?

What are your most favorite fruits?
What are your least favorite fruits?
Which of these fruits grow where you live?
Name and describe other fruits you are familiar with.

A. What do we need from the supermarket?
B. We need **lettuce*** and **pea**s.†

*1–12 †13–36

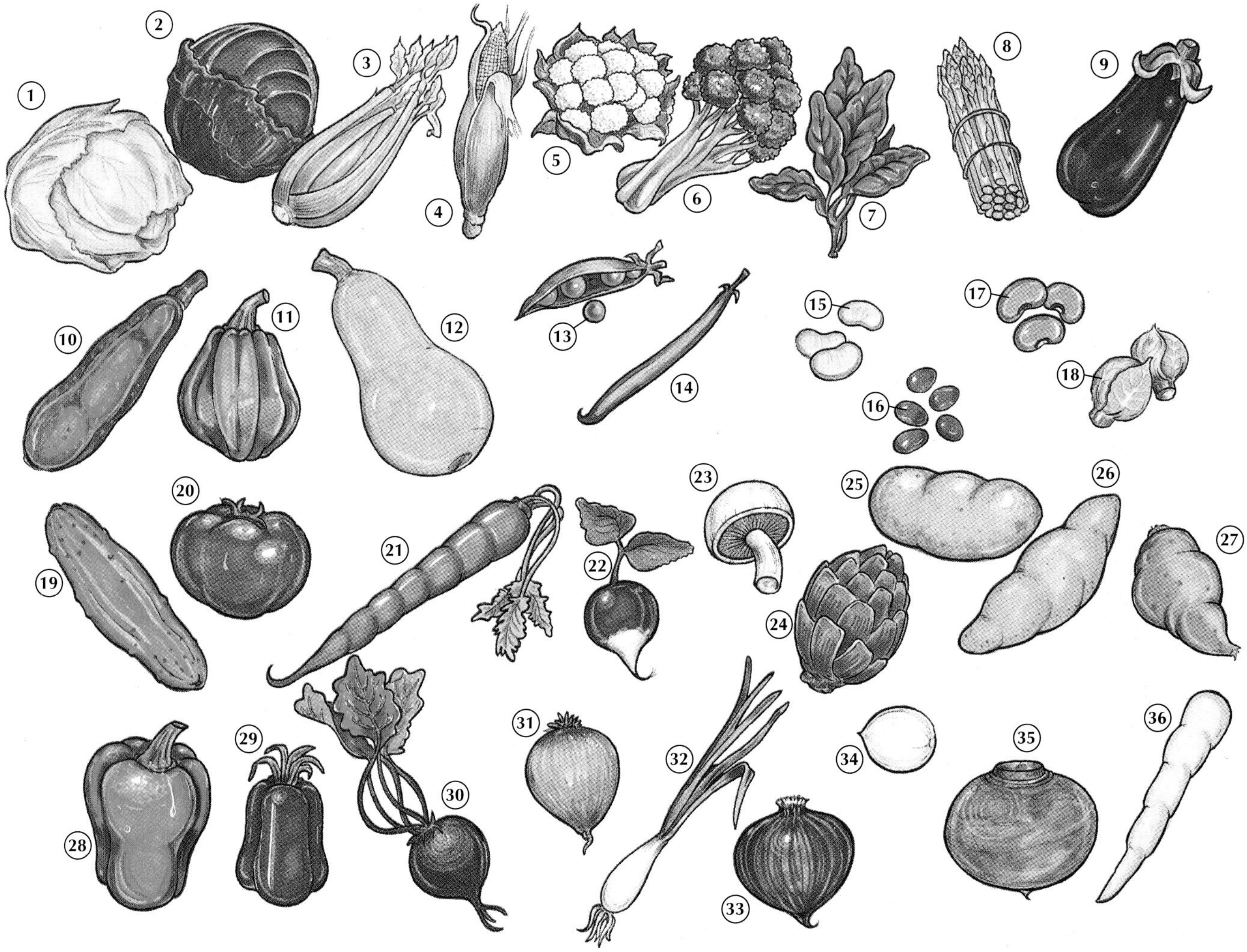

レタス **1.** lettuce
キャベツ **2.** cabbage
セロリ **3.** celery
トウモロコシ **4.** corn
カリフラワー **5.** cauliflower
ブロッコリー **6.** broccoli
ホウレンソウ **7.** spinach
アスパラガス **8.** asparagus
ナス **9.** eggplant
ズッキーニ **10.** zucchini (squash)
西洋カボチャ（どんぐり形） **11.** acorn squash
バターナットカボチャ **12.** butternut squash
エンドウ豆 **13.** pea
インゲン **14.** string bean/ green bean
ライ豆 **15.** lima bean
黒豆 **16.** black bean
ウズラ豆 **17.** kidney bean
芽キャベツ **18.** brussels sprout
キュウリ **19.** cucumber
トマト **20.** tomato
ニンジン **21.** carrot
ラディッシュ **22.** radish
マッシュルーム **23.** mushroom
アーティチョーク **24.** artichoke
ジャガイモ **25.** potato
サツマイモ **26.** sweet potato
ヤムイモ **27.** yam
ピーマン **28.** green pepper
赤ピーマン **29.** red pepper
ビーツ **30.** beet
玉ネギ **31.** onion
シャーロット/ラッキョウ/リーク **32.** scallion/ green onion
赤タマネギ **33.** red onion
小タマネギ **34.** pearl onion
カブ **35.** turnip
パースニップ（サトウニンジン） **36.** parsnip

A. How do you like the [1–12] / [13–36] s?
B. It's/They're delicious.

A. *Johnny?* Finish your vegetables!
B. But you KNOW I hate [1–12] / [13–36] s!
A. I know. But it's/they're good for you!

Which vegetables do you like?
Which vegetables don't you like?
Which of these vegetables grow where you live?
Name and describe other vegetables you are familiar with.

A. I'm going to the supermarket to get **milk** and **soup**.*
Do we need anything else?
B. Yes. We also need **cereal** and **soda**.*

**With 43, 44, 46, 49, and 55, use: a ______.*

乳製品 **A. Dairy Products**
牛乳 **1.** milk
低脂肪牛乳 **2.** low-fat milk
スキムミルク **3.** skim milk
チョコレートミルク **4.** chocolate milk
バターミルク **5.** buttermilk
オレンジジュース **6.** orange juice†
チーズ **7.** cheese
バター **8.** butter
マーガリン **9.** margarine
サワークリーム **10.** sour cream
クリームチーズ **11.** cream cheese
カッテージチーズ **12.** cottage cheese
ヨーグルト **13.** yogurt
卵 **14.** eggs

缶詰 **B. Canned Goods**
スープ **15.** soup
ツナの缶詰 **16.** tuna fish
野菜の缶詰 **17.** (canned) vegetables
果物の缶詰 **18.** (canned) fruit

箱入り食品 **C. Packaged Goods**
シリアル **19.** cereal
クッキー **20.** cookies
クラッカー **21.** crackers
スパゲティ **22.** spaghetti
めん類 **23.** noodles
マカロニ **24.** macaroni
米 **25.** rice

ジュース **D. Juice**
リンゴジュース **26.** apple juice
パイナップルジュース **27.** pineapple juice
グレープフルーツジュース **28.** grapefruit juice
トマトジュース **29.** tomato juice
フルーツパンチジュース **30.** fruit punch
グレープジュース **31.** grape juice
クランベリージュース **32.** cranberry juice
パック詰めジュース **33.** juice paks
粉末ジュース **34.** powdered drink mix

飲み物 **E. Beverages**
炭酸飲料 **35.** soda
低カロリー炭酸飲料 **36.** diet soda
飲料水/ミネラルウォーター **37.** bottled water

†オレンジジュースは乳製品ではないが，米国では通常このコーナーにある。/Orange juice is not a dairy product, but is usually found in this section.

鳥肉 **F. Poultry**

鶏肉 **38.** chicken
鶏の脚肉 **39.** chicken legs
鶏の骨付もも肉 **40.** drumsticks
鶏のむね肉 **41.** chicken breasts
鶏の手羽肉 **42.** chicken wings
七面鳥肉 **43.** turkey
鴨肉 **44.** duck

豚肉・牛肉など **G. Meat**

牛ひき肉 **45.** ground beef
ロースト用牛肉 **46.** roast
ステーキ用牛肉 **47.** steak
シチュー用牛肉 **48.** stewing meat
子羊の脚肉 **49.** leg of lamb
子羊の厚切り肉(ラムチャップ) **50.** lamb chops
豚肉 **51.** pork
豚の厚切り肉(ポークチャップ) **52.** pork chops
豚のあばら肉(スペアリブ) **53.** ribs
ソーセージ **54.** sausages
ハム **55.** ham
ベーコン **56.** bacon

海産食品 **H. Seafood**

魚 FISH

サケ **57.** salmon
ヒラメ **58.** halibut
カレイ **59.** flounder
メカジキ **60.** swordfish
タラ **61.** haddock
マス **62.** trout

貝および甲殻類 SHELLFISH

カキ **63.** oysters
ホタテ貝 **64.** scallops
小エビ **65.** shrimp
ムール貝 **66.** mussels
ハマグリ **67.** clams
カニ **68.** crabs
イセエビ **69.** lobster

パン類 **I. Baked Goods**

イングリッシュマフィン **70.** English muffins
ケーキ **71.** cake
ピタパン **72.** pita bread
ロールパン **73.** rolls
食パン **74.** bread

冷凍食品 **J. Frozen Foods**

アイスクリーム **75.** ice cream
冷凍野菜 **76.** frozen vegetables
冷凍総菜 **77.** frozen dinners
冷凍レモネード **78.** frozen lemonade
冷凍オレンジジュース **79.** frozen orange juice

A. Excuse me. Where can I find [1–79] ?
B. In the [A–J] Section, next to the [1–79] .
A. Thank you.

A. Pardon me. I'm looking for [1–79] .
B. It's/They're in the [A–J] Section, between the [1–79] and the [1–79] .
A. Thanks.

Which of these foods do you like?
Which foods are good for you?
What brands of these foods do you buy?

[1–70]
A. Look! ________ is/are on sale this week!
B. Let's get some!

総菜 **A. Deli**
- ローストビーフ **1.** roast beef
- ボローニャソーセージ **2.** bologna
- サラミ **3.** salami
- ハム **4.** ham
- 七面鳥 **5.** turkey
- コンビーフ **6.** corned beef
- アメリカンチーズ **7.** American cheese
- スイスチーズ **8.** Swiss cheese
- イタリアンチーズ **9.** provolone
- モッツァレラチーズ **10.** mozzarella
- チェダーチーズ **11.** cheddar cheese
- ポテトサラダ **12.** potato salad
- コールスロー（キャベツサラダ） **13.** cole slaw
- マカロニサラダ **14.** macaroni salad
- シーフードサラダ **15.** seafood salad

菓子 **B. Snack Foods**
- ポテトチップス **16.** potato chips
- コーンチップス **17.** corn chips
- トルティーヤチップス **18.** tortilla chips
- ナッチョチップス **19.** nacho chips
- プリッツェル **20.** pretzels
- ポップコーン **21.** popcorn
- 木の実類 **22.** nuts
- ピーナッツ **23.** peanuts

調味料 **C. Condiments**
- ケチャップ **24.** ketchup
- からし **25.** mustard
- 薬味 **26.** relish
- ピクルス **27.** pickles
- オリーブ **28.** olives
- 塩 **29.** salt
- こしょう **30.** pepper
- 香辛料 **31.** spices
- しょう油 **32.** soy sauce
- マヨネーズ **33.** mayonnaise
- 料理用油 **34.** (cooking) oil
- オリーブ油 **35.** olive oil
- 酢 **36.** vinegar
- ドレッシング **37.** salad dressing

コーヒー・紅茶 **D. Coffee and Tea**
- コーヒー **38.** coffee
- カフェイン抜きコーヒー **39.** decaffeinated coffee/ decaf coffee
- 紅茶 **40.** tea
- ハーブティー（薬草茶） **41.** herbal tea
- ココア **42.** cocoa/ hot chocolate mix

製菓材 **E. Baking Products**
- 小麦粉 **43.** flour
- 砂糖 **44.** sugar
- ケーキの素 **45.** cake mix

ジャム・ゼリー **F. Jams and Jellies**
ジャム **46.** jam
ゼリー状のジャム **47.** jelly
マーマレード **48.** marmalade
ピーナッツバター **49.** peanut butter

紙製品 **G. Paper Products**
ティッシュペーパー **50.** tissues
ナプキン **51.** napkins
トイレットペーパー **52.** toilet paper
紙コップ **53.** paper cups
紙皿 **54.** paper plates
ストロー **55.** straws
ペーパータオル **56.** paper towels

家庭用品 **H. Household Items**
サンドイッチ入れ/弁当箱 **57.** sandwich bags
ゴミ袋 **58.** trash bags
石けん **59.** soap
液体石けん **60.** liquid soap
アルミホイル **61.** aluminum foil
ラップ **62.** plastic wrap
ろう紙 **63.** waxed paper

ベビー用品 **I. Baby Products**
ベビーシリアル **64.** baby cereal
乳児用人工乳 **65.** formula
ベビーフード **66.** baby food
おしり拭き **67.** wipes
紙おむつ **68.** (disposable) diapers

ペットフード **J. Pet Food**
キャットフード **69.** cat food
ドッグフード **70.** dog food

レジ **K. Checkout Area**
通路 **71.** aisle
ショッピングカート **72.** shopping cart
買物客 **73.** shopper/customer
レジ台 **74.** checkout counter
ベルトコンベア **75.** conveyor belt
クーポン券 **76.** coupons
スキャナー **77.** scanner
はかり **78.** scale
レジ **79.** cash register
レジ係 **80.** cashier
ポリ袋 **81.** plastic bag
紙袋 **82.** paper bag
袋詰め係 **83.** bagger/packer
エキスプレスレジ (買物量の少ない人用のレジ) **84.** express checkout (line)
タブロイド判新聞 **85.** tabloid (newspaper)
雑誌 **86.** magazine
ガム **87.** (chewing) gum
あめ **88.** candy
店内用かご **89.** shopping basket

A. Do we need [1–70] ?
B. No, but we need [1–70] .

A. We forgot to get [1–70] !
B. I'll get it/them.
Where is it?/Where are they?
A. In the [A–J] Section over there.

Make a complete shopping list of everything you need from the supermarket.
Describe the differences between U.S. supermarkets and food stores in your country.

A. Would you please get a **bag** of *flour* when you go to the supermarket?
B. A **bag** of *flour?* Sure. I'd be happy to.

A. Would you please get two **head**s of *lettuce* when you go to the supermarket?
B. Two **head**s of *lettuce?* Sure. I'd be happy to.

袋 **1.** bag
(チョコレート・石けんなど板状のもの)個/枚 **2.** bar
びん/本 **3.** bottle
箱 **4.** box
ふさ **5.** bunch
かん **6.** can
(牛乳など) パック **7.** carton
(容器入り食品) 個 **8.** container
ダース (12個) **9.** dozen*
(トウモロコシなど) 本 **10.** ear
(キャベツ, レタスなど) 個 **11.** head
(ジャムなど) びん **12.** jar

* "a dozen of eggs" ではなく "a dozen eggs"。/ "a dozen eggs," NOT "a dozen of eggs."

（パンなど）個 **13.** loaf-loaves
（ガム・タバコなど）包み **14.** pack
包み/パック **15.** package
巻き **16.** roll
（ビールなど）半ダースカートン **17.** six-pack

（バターなど棒状のもの）個 **18.** stick
（容器に入ったマーガリンなど）個 **19.** tub
1パイント容器 **20.** pint
（約0.473ℓ*，1/2quart）
1クォート容器 **21.** quart
（約0.946ℓ*，1/4gallon）

1/2ガロン容器 **22.** half-gallon
1ガロン容器 **23.** gallon
（3.785ℓ*）
1リットル容器 **24.** liter
1ポンド（約0.4536kg） **25.** pound

*米国式換算

[At home]
A. What did you get at the supermarket?
B. I got ________, ________, and ________.

[In a supermarket]
A. Is this checkout counter open?
B. Yes, but this is the express line. Do you have more than eight items?
B. No. I only have ________, ________, and ________.

Open your kitchen cabinets and refrigerator. Make a list of all the things you find.
What do you do with empty bottles, jars, and cans? Do you recycle them, reuse them, or throw them away?

teaspoon (tsp.)
ティースプーン(小さじ)

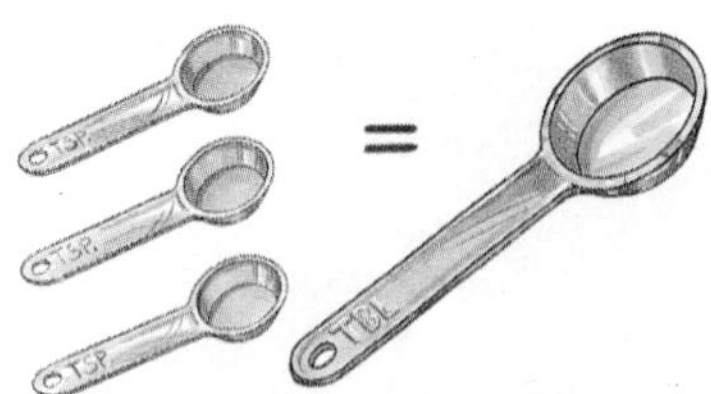

tablespoon (Tbsp.)
テーブルスプーン(大さじ)

1 (fluid) ounce (1 fl. oz.)
1(液状)オンス

cup
カップ
=8 fl. ozs.
8(液状)オンス

pint (pt.) パイント
=16 fl. ozs.
16(液状)オンス

quart (qt.) クォート
=32 fl. ozs.
32(液状)オンス

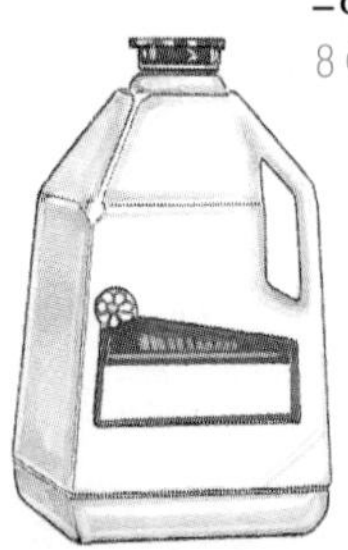

gallon (gal.) ガロン
=128 fl. ozs.
128(液状)オンス

A. How much water should I put in?
B. The recipe says to add one ________ of water.

A. This fruit punch is delicious! What's in it?
B. Two ________s of orange juice, three ________s of grape juice, and a ________ of apple juice.

an ounce (oz.)
1オンス

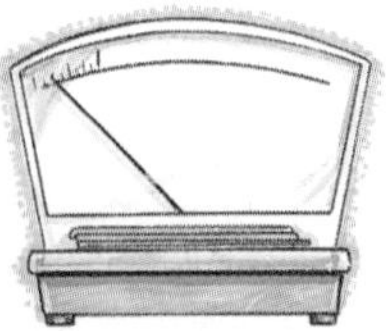

a quarter of a pound (¼ lb.)
¼ポンド
=4 ozs.
4オンス

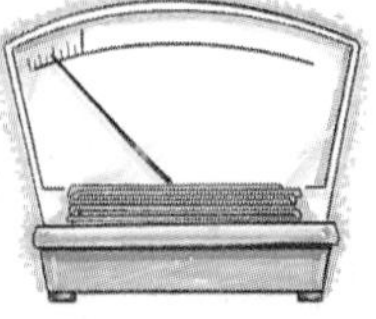

half a pound (½ lb.)
½ポンド
=8 ozs.
8オンス

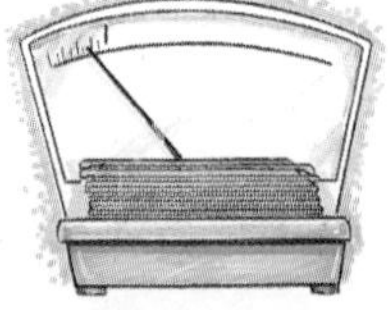

three-quarters of a pound (¾ lb.)
¾ポンド
=12 ozs.
12オンス

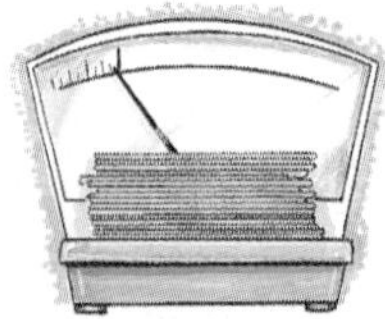

a pound (lb.)
1ポンド
=16 ozs.
16オンス

A. How much roast beef would you like?
B. I'd like ________, please.

A. This chili tastes very good! What did you put in it?
B. ________ of ground beef, ________ of beans, ________ of tomatoes, and ________ of chili powder.

A. Can I help?
B. Yes. Please **cut up** the *vegetables*.

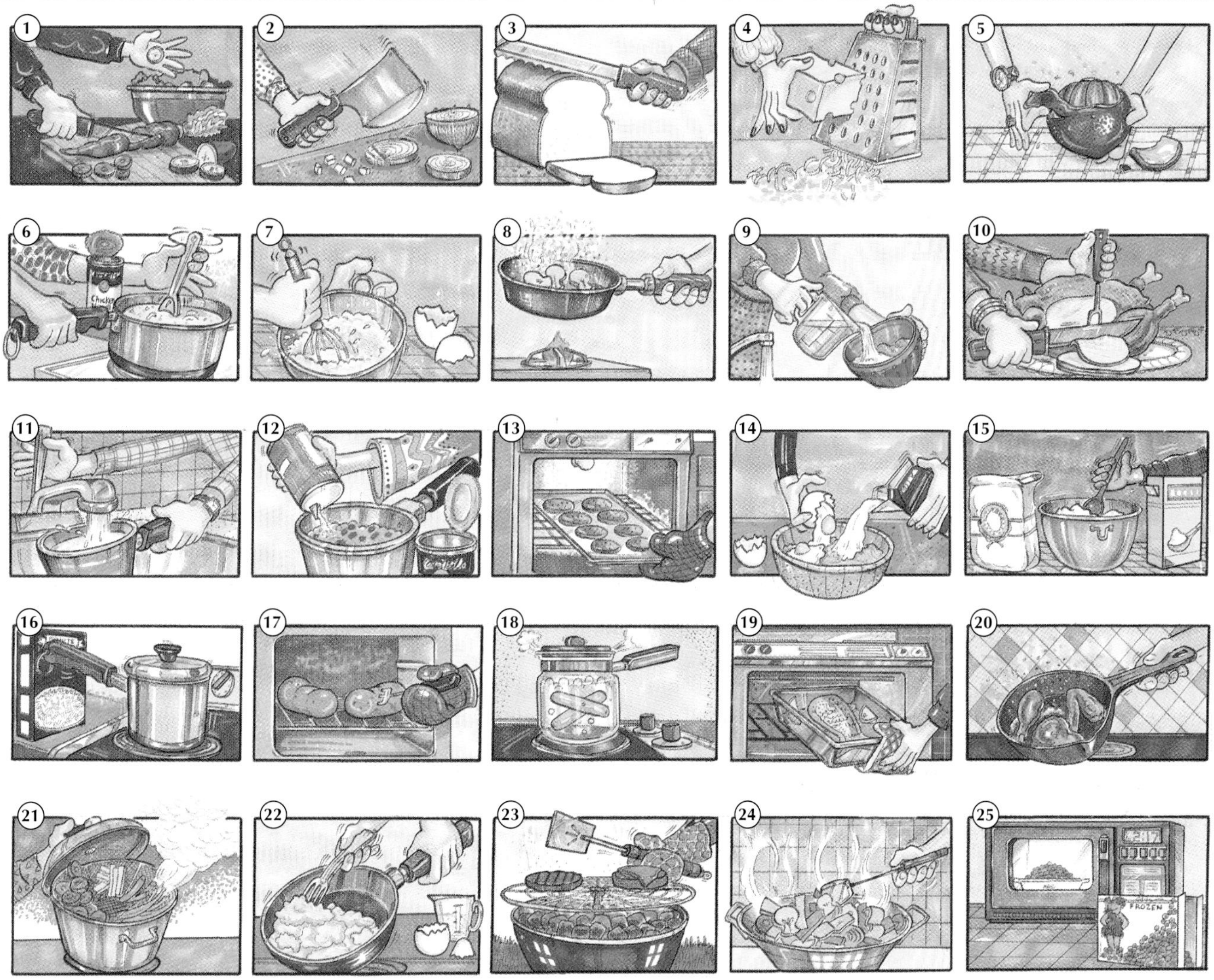

切る **1.** cut (up)
ぶつ切りにする **2.** chop (up)
薄く切る **3.** slice
すりおろす **4.** grate
皮をむく **5.** peel
かきまわす **6.** stir
強くかきまぜる **7.** beat
手早くいためる **8.** saute
注ぐ **9.** pour
切り分ける **10.** carve
AにBをいっぱいに入れる **11.** fill A with B
AをBに加える **12.** add A to B
AをBに入れる **13.** put A in B
AとBを合わせる **14.** combine A and B
AとBを合わせてかきまぜる **15.** mix A and B
加熱して料理する **16.** cook
天火で焼く **17.** bake
ゆでる **18.** boil
直火で焼く **19.** broil
いためる/揚げる **20.** fry
蒸す **21.** steam
かきまぜながら焼く **22.** scramble
網焼きする **23.** barbecue/grill
かきまぜながらいためる **24.** stir-fry
電子レンジで調理する **25.** microwave

[1–25] A. What are you doing?
B. I'm ________ing the ....

[16–25] A. How long should I ________ the ....?
B. For .... minutes/seconds.

What's your favorite recipe? Give instructions and use the units of measure on page 52. For example:
Mix a cup of flour and two tablespoons of sugar.
Add half a pound of butter.
Bake at 350° (degrees) for twenty minutes.

ドーナツ	**1.** donut	コカコーラ・低カロリーコーラ・ペプシコーラ・セブンナップなど	**15.** Coke/Diet Coke/ Pepsi/7-Up/...	ローストビーフサンドイッチ	**26.** roast beef sandwich
マフィン	**2.** muffin	レモネード	**16.** lemonade	コンビーフサンドイッチ	**27.** corned beef sandwich
ベーグル	**3.** bagel	コーヒー	**17.** coffee	BLT(ベーコン・レタス・トマトの)サンドイッチ	**28.** BLT/bacon, lettuce,and tomato sandwich
パン	**4.** bun	カフェイン抜きコーヒー	**18.** decaf coffee	精白パン	**29.** white bread
ペストリー	**5.** danish/pastry	紅茶	**19.** tea	ライ麦パン	**30.** rye bread
ビスケット/スコーン	**6.** biscuit	アイスティー	**20.** iced tea	全麦パン	**31.** whole wheat bread
クロワッサン	**7.** croissant	牛乳	**21.** milk	(粗製の)ライ麦パン	**32.** pumpernickel
ハンバーガー	**8.** hamburger	ツナサンドイッチ	**22.** tuna fish sandwich	ピタパン	**33.** pita bread
チーズバーガー	**9.** cheeseburger	卵サンドイッチ	**23.** egg salad sandwich	ロールパン	**34.** a roll
ホットドッグ	**10.** hot dog	チキンサンドイッチ	**24.** chicken salad sandwich	サブマリンロールパン	**35.** a submarine roll
タコス	**11.** taco	ハムとチーズのサンドイッチ	**25.** ham and cheese sandwich		
ピザ	**12.** slice of pizza				
チリコンカルネ	**13.** bowl of chili				
フライドチキン	**14.** order of fried chicken				

A. May I help you?
B. Yes. I'd like a/an [1–14], please.
A. Anything to drink?
B. Yes. I'll have a small/medium-size/ large/extra-large [15–21].

A. I'd like a [22–28] on [29–35], please.
B. What do you want on it?
A. Lettuce/tomato/mayonnaise/mustard/...

Do you go to fast food restaurants or sandwich shops? When? How often? What do you order?

前菜 A. Appetizers

- フルーツカクテル **1.** fruit cup/ fruit cocktail
- トマトジュース **2.** tomato juice
- 小エビのカクテル **3.** shrimp cocktail
- 鳥の手羽焼 **4.** chicken wings
- ナッチョス **5.** nachos
- ポテトスキン **6.** potato skins

サラダ B. Salads

- グリーンサラダ **7.** tossed salad/ garden salad
- ギリシア風サラダ **8.** Greek salad
- ホウレンソウサラダ **9.** spinach salad
- アンティパスト **10.** antipasto (plate)
- シーザーサラダ **11.** Caesar salad
- サラダバー **12.** salad bar

主菜 C. Main Courses/Entrees

- ミートローフ **13.** meatloaf
- ローストビーフ/プライムリブ **14.** roast beef/ prime rib
- 子牛のカツレツ **15.** veal cutlet
- 鶏の丸焼き **16.** baked chicken
- 焼き魚 **17.** broiled fish
- スパゲティミートボール **18.** spaghetti and meatballs

副菜 D. Side Dishes

- ベークドポテト **19.** baked potato
- マッシュポテト **20.** mashed potatoes
- フライドポテト **21.** french fries
- 米 **22.** rice
- パスタ **23.** noodles
- ミックスベジタブル **24.** mixed vegetables

デザート E. Desserts

- チョコレートケーキ **25.** chocolate cake
- アップルパイ **26.** apple pie
- アイスクリーム **27.** ice cream
- フルーツゼリー **28.** jello
- プリン **29.** pudding
- サンデー/パフェ **30.** ice cream sundae

[Ordering dinner]

A. May I take your order?
B. Yes, please. For the appetizer I'd like the [1–6].
A. And what kind of salad would you like?
B. I'll have the [7–12].
A. And for the main course?
B. I'd like the [13–18], please.
A. What side dish would you like with that?
B. Hmm. I think I'll have [19–24].

[Ordering dessert]

A. Would you care for some dessert?
B. Yes. I'll have [25–29] /an [30].

Do you go to restaurants? Which ones? What do you order? Describe some popular desserts in your country.

A. What's your favorite color?
B. **Red.**

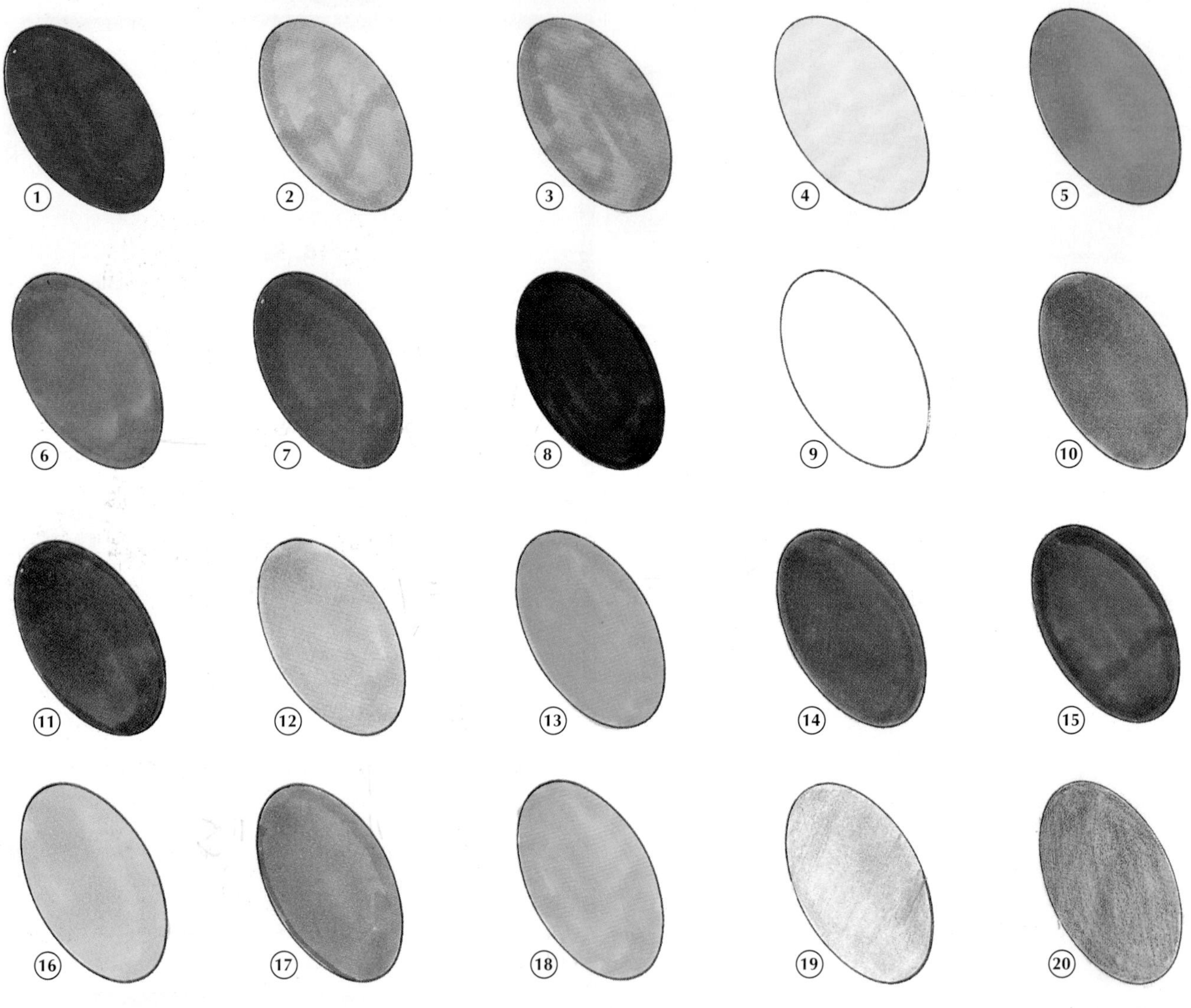

1	2	3	4	5
6	7	8	9	10
11	12	13	14	15
16	17	18	19	20

赤 **1.** red
ピンク **2.** pink
だいだい色 **3.** orange
黄色 **4.** yellow
緑 **5.** green
青 **6.** blue
紫 **7.** purple

黒 **8.** black
白 **9.** white
灰色 **10.** gray
茶色 **11.** brown
ベージュ **12.** beige
黄緑 **13.** light green
深緑 **14.** dark green

紺色 **15.** navy blue
青緑 **16.** turquoise
ホットピンク **17.** hot pink
ネオングリーン **18.** neon green
銀色 **19.** silver
金色 **20.** gold

A. I like your _______ shirt.
You look very good in _______.
B. Thank you. _______ is my favorite color.

A. My color TV is broken.
B. What's the matter with it?
A. People's faces are _______, the sky is _______, and the grass is _______!

Do you know the flags of different countries? What are the colors of the flags you know?
What color makes you happy? What color makes you sad? Why?

A. I think I'll wear my new **shirt** today.
B. Good idea!

(長そで) シャツ	**1.** shirt/long-sleeved shirt	コーデュロイのズボン	**11.** corduroy pants/ corduroys	カジュアルジャケット	**21.** jacket/sports jacket/ sports coat
半そでシャツ	**2.** short-sleeved shirt	スカート	**12.** skirt	上着	**22.** jacket
ワイシャツ	**3.** dress shirt	ワンピース	**13.** dress	ブレザー	**23.** blazer
カジュアルシャツ	**4.** sport shirt	ジャンプスーツ	**14.** jumpsuit	スーツ	**24.** suit
ポロシャツ	**5.** polo shirt/jersey/ sport shirt	ショートパンツ (半ズボン)	**15.** shorts	三つ揃いの背広	**25.** three-piece suit
ネルのシャツ	**6.** flannel shirt	セーター	**16.** sweater	ベスト	**26.** vest
ブラウス	**7.** blouse	Vネックのセーター	**17.** V-neck sweater	ネクタイ	**27.** tie/necktie
タートルネック (のセーター)	**8.** turtleneck	カーディガン	**18.** cardigan sweater	蝶ネクタイ	**28.** bowtie
ズボン	**9.** pants/slacks	オーバーオール	**19.** overalls	タキシード	**29.** tuxedo
ジーンズ	**10.** (blue) jeans	制服	**20.** uniform	イブニングドレス	**30.** (evening) gown

A. I really like your ______.
B. Thank you.
A. Where did you get it/them?
B. At ....

A. Oh, no! I just ripped my ______!
B. What a shame!

What color clothes do you like to wear?
Do you ever wear jeans? When?
What do you wear at parties? at work or at school? at weddings?

パジャマ **1.** pajamas
ネグリジェ/ねまき **2.** nightgown
シャツねまき **3.** nightshirt
バスローブ **4.** bathrobe/robe
スリッパ **5.** slippers
肌着/Tシャツ **6.** undershirt/ tee shirt
ブリーフ **7.** (jockey) shorts/ underpants
トランクス **8.** boxer shorts
サポーター **9.** athletic supporter/ jock strap
防寒用肌着 **10.** long underwear/ long johns
(ビキニ型) ショーツ **11.** (bikini) panties/ underpants
ショーツ **12.** briefs
ブラジャー **13.** bra
キャミソール **14.** camisole
スリップ **15.** slip
ペチコート **16.** half slip
ストッキング **17.** stockings
パンティーストッキング **18.** pantyhose
タイツ **19.** tights
くつ下 **20.** socks
ハイソックス **21.** knee socks
靴 **22.** shoes
ハイヒール **23.** (high) heels
パンプス **24.** pumps
ローファー **25.** loafers
スニーカー **26.** sneakers
テニスシューズ **27.** tennis shoes
ジョギングシューズ **28.** running shoes
ハイカット **29.** high tops/
バスケットシューズ high-top sneakers
サンダル **30.** sandals
ビーチサンダル **31.** thongs/flip-flops
ブーツ **32.** boots
ワーキングブーツ **33.** work boots
登山靴 **34.** hiking boots
カウボーイブーツ **35.** cowboy boots
モカシン **36.** moccasins

[1–21] A. I can't find my new ________.
B. Did you look in the bureau/dresser/closet?
A. Yes, I did.
B. Then it's/they're probably in the wash.

[22–36] A. Are those new ________?
B. Yes, they are.
A. They're very nice.
B. Thanks.

Tシャツ	1.	tee shirt
タンクトップ	2.	tank top
スエットシャツ（トレーナー）	3.	sweatshirt
スエットパンツ	4.	sweat pants
ジョギングパンツ	5.	running shorts
テニス用ショートパンツ	6.	tennis shorts
ライクラパンツ	7.	lycra shorts
ジョギングスーツ	8.	jogging suit/ running suit
レオタード	9.	leotard
タイツ	10.	tights
スエットバンド	11.	sweatband
コート	12.	coat
オーバーコート	13.	overcoat
ジャケット	14.	jacket
ウインドブレーカー	15.	windbreaker
スキー用ジャケット	16.	ski jacket
ボンバージャケット	17.	bomber jacket
アノラック	18.	parka
ダウンジャケット	19.	down jacket
ダウンベスト	20.	down vest
レインコート	21.	raincoat
ポンチョ	22.	poncho
トレンチコート	23.	trenchcoat
オーバーシューズ	24.	rubbers
手袋	25.	gloves
ミトン	26.	mittens
（縁のある）帽子	27.	hat
（縁のない）帽子	28.	cap
野球帽	29.	baseball cap
ベレー帽	30.	beret
レインハット	31.	rain hat
スキー帽	32.	ski hat
スキーマスク	33.	ski mask
耳当て	34.	ear muffs
マフラー	35.	scarf

[1–11] A. Excuse me. I found this/these ______ in the dryer. Is it/Are they yours?
B. Yes. It's/They're mine. Thank you.

[12–35] A. What's the weather like today?
B. It's cool/cold/raining/snowing.
A. I think I'll wear my ______.

Do you exercise? How? What kind of clothing and shoes do you wear when you exercise?

What do you wear outside when the weather is bad?

A. Oh, no! I think I lost my **ring**!
B. I'll help you look for it.

A. Oh, no! I think I lost my **earrings**!
B. I'll help you look for them.

指輪 **1.** ring
婚約指輪 **2.** engagement ring
結婚指輪 **3.** wedding ring/ wedding band
イヤリング **4.** earrings
ネックレス **5.** necklace
真珠のネックレス **6.** pearl necklace/ pearls
鎖 **7.** chain
ビーズ（のネックレス） **8.** beads
ブローチ **9.** pin
腕時計 **10.** watch/ wrist watch
ブレスレット **11.** bracelet
カフスボタン **12.** cuff links
ネクタイピン **13.** tie pin/ tie tack
タイ留め **14.** tie clip
ベルト **15.** belt
キーホルダー **16.** key ring/ key chain
財布 **17.** wallet
小銭入れ **18.** change purse
ハンドバッグ **19.** pocketbook/ purse/handbag
ショルダーバッグ **20.** shoulder bag
手さげかばん **21.** tote bag
ランドセル式かばん **22.** book bag
リュックサック/デイパック **23.** backpack
書類かばん/ブリーフケース **24.** briefcase
傘 **25.** umbrella

[In a store]
A. Excuse me. Is this/Are these ________ on sale this week?
B. Yes. It's/They're half price.

[On the street]
A. Help! Police! Stop that man/woman!
B. What happened?!
A. He/She just stole my ________ and my ________!

Do you like to wear jewelry? What jewelry do you have?
In your country, what do men, women, and children use to carry their things?

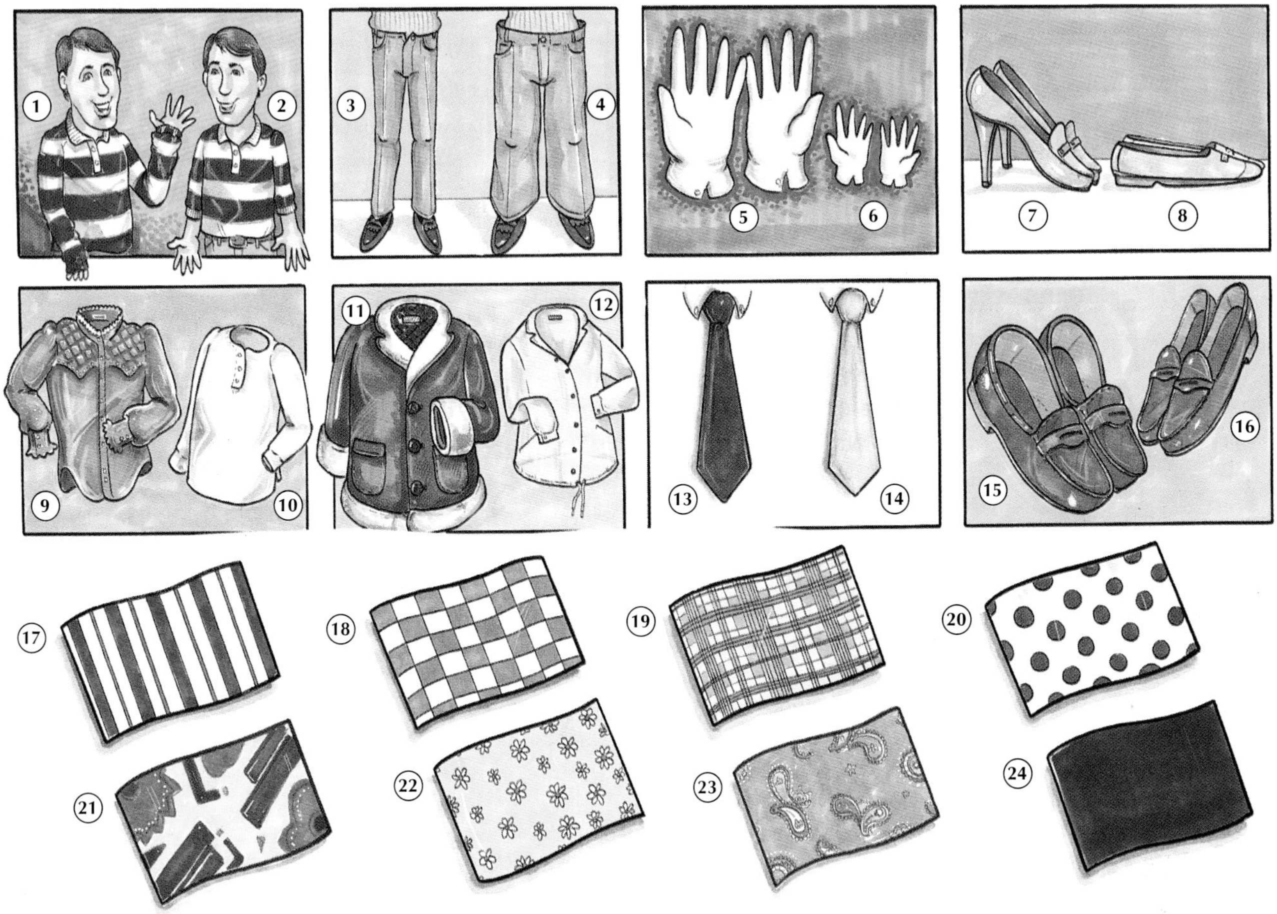

長い－短い **1- 2** long-short
ぴったりした－ゆるい **3- 4** tight-loose/baggy
大きい－小さい **5- 6** large/big-small
高い－低い **7- 8** high-low
はでな－地味な **9-10** fancy-plain
厚手の－薄手の **11-12** heavy-light

（色が）暗い－明るい **13-14** dark-light
広い－狭い **15-16** wide-narrow
しま模様の **17.** striped
市松模様の **18.** checked
格子柄の **19.** plaid

水玉模様の **20.** polka dot
プリント柄の **21.** print
花模様の **22.** flowered
ペイズリー模様の **23.** paisley
青い無地の **24.** solid blue

[1–2]
A. Are the sleeves too **long**?
B. No. They're too **short**.

1–2	Are the sleeves too ______?	9–10	Is the blouse too ______?
3–4	Are the pants too ______?	11–12	Is the coat too ______?
5–6	Are the gloves too ______?	13–14	Is the color too ______?
7–8	Are the heels too ______?	15–16	Are the shoes too ______?

[17–24]
A. How do you like this _______ tie/shirt/skirt?
B. Actually, I prefer that _______ one.

Describe your favorite clothing.

A. Excuse me. Where's the **store directory**?
B. It's over there, next to the **escalator**.

売場案内 **1.** (store) directory
エスカレーター **2.** escalator
紳士服売場 **3.** Men's Clothing Department
香水売場 **4.** Perfume Counter
宝石売場 **5.** Jewelry Counter
エレベーター **6.** elevator
男子トイレ **7.** men's room
女子トイレ **8.** ladies' room
水飲み場 **9.** water fountain
パーキングビル **10.** parking garage
婦人服売場 **11.** Women's Clothing Department
子供服売場 **12.** Children's Clothing Department
家庭用品売場 **13.** Housewares Department
家具売場 **14.** Furniture Department/ Home Furnishings Department
家庭用電化製品売場 **15.** Household Appliances Department
テレビ・音響製品売場 **16.** Electronics Department
お客様サービスカウンター **17.** Customer Assistance Counter/ Customer Service Counter
スナック（軽食）スタンド **18.** snack bar
贈答品包装カウンター **19.** Gift Wrap Counter
駐車場 **20.** parking lot
商品受取所 **21.** customer pickup area

A. Pardon me. Is this the way to the _______?
B. Yes, it is./No, it isn't.

A. I'll meet you at/in/near/in front of the _______.
B. Okay. What time?
A. At *3:00*.

Describe a department store you know. Tell what is on each floor.

A. May I help you?
B. Yes, please. I'm looking for a **TV**.

テレビ	**1.**	TV/television set
リモコン	**2.**	remote control (unit)
ビデオデッキ	**3.**	VCR/videocassette recorder
(未録画)ビデオテープ	**4.**	(blank) videotape
ビデオテープ	**5.**	video/(video) tape
ビデオカメラ	**6.**	camcorder/videocamera
レコードプレーヤー	**7.**	turntable
テープデッキ	**8.**	tape deck
CDプレーヤー	**9.**	CD player/compact disc player
アンプ	**10.**	amplifier
チューナー	**11.**	tuner
スピーカー	**12.**	speaker
ステレオ	**13.**	stereo system/sound system
テープレコーダー	**14.**	tape recorder
ヘッドフォンステレオ/ウォークマン	**15.**	(personal) cassette player/Walkman
ミニコンポ	**16.**	portable stereo system/boom box
カセットテープ	**17.**	(audio) tape/(audio)cassette
CD(コンパクトディスク)	**18.**	CD/compact disc
レコード	**19.**	record
ヘッドホン	**20.**	set of headphones
ラジオ	**21.**	radio
短波ラジオ	**22.**	shortwave radio
タイマー付ラジオ	**23.**	clock radio

A. How do you like my ________?
B. It's great/fantastic/awesome!

A. Which company makes a good ________?
B. In my opinion, the best ________ is made by ....

What video and audio equipment do you have or want?
In your opinion, which brands are the best?

A. Can you recommend a good **computer**?*
B. Yes. This **computer** here is excellent.

- コンピューター **1.** computer
- モニター **2.** monitor
- ディスクドライブ **3.** disk drive
- キーボード **4.** keyboard
- マウス **5.** mouse
- プリンター **6.** printer
- モデム **7.** modem
- フロッピーディスク **8.** (floppy) disk/diskette
- ソフトウエア **9.** (computer) software
- 小型コンピューター **10.** portable computer
- ノート型コンピューター **11.** notebook computer
- 電話機 **12.** telephone/phone
- コードレス電話機 **13.** portable phone /portable telephone
- 留守番電話 **14.** answering machine
- ファクシミリ **15.** fax machine
- カメラ **16.** camera
- ズームレンズ **17.** zoom lens
- カメラケース **18.** camera case
- フラッシュ **19.** flash attachment
- 三脚 **20.** tripod
- フィルム **21.** film
- スライド映写機 **22.** slide projector
- スクリーン **23.** (movie) screen
- 電動タイプライター **24.** electric typewriter
- 電子タイプライター **25.** electronic typewriter
- 電卓 **26.** calculator
- 計算器 **27.** adding machine
- レギュレーター（電圧調整器） **28.** voltage regulator
- アダプター **29.** adapter

A. Excuse me. Do you sell _______s?†
B. Yes. We carry a complete line of _______s.†

†*With 9 and 21, use the singular.*

A. Which _______ is the best?
B. This one here. It's made by …………

Do you have a camera? What kind is it? What do you take pictures of?
Does anyone you know have an answering machine? When you call, what does the machine say?
How have computers changed the world?

A. Excuse me. I'm looking for (a/an) ________(s) for my *grandson.**
B. Look in the next aisle.
A. Thank you.

* *grandson/granddaughter/...*

卓上ゲーム/ゲーム盤	**1.**	(board) game
積み木	**2.**	(building) blocks
工作セット	**3.**	construction set
ジグソーパズル	**4.**	(jigsaw) puzzle
ゴムまり	**5.**	rubber ball
ビーチボール	**6.**	beach ball
バケツとシャベル	**7.**	pail and shovel
フラフープ	**8.**	hula hoop
なわとび	**9.**	jump rope
人形	**10.**	doll
着せ替え人形の洋服	**11.**	doll clothing
ドールハウス（ミニチュアの家）	**12.**	doll house
ドールハウスの家具	**13.**	doll house furniture
アクション人形	**14.**	action figure
ぬいぐるみ	**15.**	stuffed animal
ミニカー	**16.**	matchbox car
オモチャのトラック	**17.**	toy truck
レーシングカーセット	**18.**	racing car set
電車セット	**19.**	train set
プラモデル	**20.**	model kit
実験セット	**21.**	science kit
クレヨン	**22.**	crayons
サインペン	**23.**	(color) markers
ぬり絵	**24.**	coloring book
（図工用）色画用紙	**25.**	construction paper
絵の具セット	**26.**	paint set
粘土	**27.**	(modeling) clay
自転車	**28.**	bicycle
三輪車	**29.**	tricycle
四輪車	**30.**	wagon
スケートボード	**31.**	skateboard
ブランコ	**32.**	swing set
ビニールプール	**33.**	plastic swimming pool/ wading pool
テレビゲーム	**34.**	video game system
テレビゲームソフト	**35.**	(video) game cartridge
携帯用テレビゲーム	**36.**	hand-held video game
携帯用無線電話機	**37.**	walkie-talkie (set)
トレーディングカード（野球カードなど）	**38.**	trading cards
シール	**39.**	stickers
シャボン玉	**40.**	bubble soap
おもちゃの家	**41.**	play house

A. I don't know what to get my ....-year-old son/daughter for his/her birthday.
B. What about (a) ________?
A. Good idea! Thanks.

A. Mom/Dad? Can we buy this/these ________?
B. No, *Johnny*. Not today.

What toys are most popular in your country?
What were your favorite toys when you were a child?

硬貨/Coins

名称	Name	価値	Value	表記	Written as:
ペニー	**1.** penny	1セント	one cent	1¢	$ .01
ニッケル	**2.** nickel	5セント	five cents	5¢	$ .05
ダイム	**3.** dime	10セント	ten cents	10¢	$ .10
クォーター	**4.** quarter	25セント	twenty-five cents	25¢	$ .25
ハーフダラー	**5.** half dollar	50セント	fifty cents	50¢	$ .50
シルバーダラー	**6.** silver dollar	1ドル	one dollar		$1.00

A. How much is a **penny** worth?
B. A penny is worth **one cent**.

A. *Soda* costs *seventy-five cents.*
Do you have enough change?
B. Yes. I have a/two/three ______(s) and . . . .

通貨紙幣/Currency

名称	Name	通称	We sometimes say:	価値	Value	表記	Written as:
1ドル紙幣	**7.** (one-)dollar bill		a one	1ドル	one dollar		$ 1.00
5ドル紙幣	**8.** five-dollar bill		a five	5ドル	five dollars		$ 5.00
10ドル紙幣	**9.** ten-dollar bill		a ten	10ドル	ten dollars		$ 10.00
20ドル紙幣	**10.** twenty-dollar bill		a twenty	20ドル	twenty dollars		$ 20.00
50ドル紙幣	**11.** fifty-dollar bill		a fifty	50ドル	fifty dollars		$ 50.00
100ドル紙幣	**12.** (one-)hundred dollar bill		a hundred	100ドル	one hundred dollars		$100.00

A. I need to go to the supermarket.
Do you have any cash?
B. Let me see. I have a **twenty-dollar bill**.
A. **Twenty dollars** is enough. Thanks.

A. Can you change a **five-dollar bill/a five**?
B. Yes. I've got ***five* one-dollar bills/*five* ones**.

Written as	*We say:*
$1.20	one dollar and twenty cents a dollar twenty
$2.50	two dollars and fifty cents two fifty
$37.43	thirty-seven dollars and forty-three cents thirty-seven forty-three

How much do you pay for a loaf of bread? a hamburger? a cup of coffee? a gallon of gas?
Name and describe the coins and currency in your country. What are they worth in U.S. dollars?

小切手帳 **1.** checkbook	キャッシュカード **7.** ATM card	貸金庫 **14.** safe deposit box
小切手記録簿 **2.** check register	預金伝票 **8.** deposit slip	金銭出納係 **15.** teller
月々の利用明細書 **3.** monthly statement	払戻伝票 **9.** withdrawal slip	警備員 **16.** security guard
通帳 **4.** bank book	小切手 **10.** check	自動預払機 **17.** automatic teller (machine)/ ATM (machine)
トラベラーズチェック (旅行者用小切手) **5.** traveler's checks	為替 **11.** money order	行員 **18.** bank officer
クレジットカード **6.** credit card	貸付申請書 **12.** loan application	
	金庫 **13.** (bank) vault	

[1–7]
A. What are you looking for?
B. My ________. I can't find it/them anywhere!

[8–12]
A. What are you doing?
B. I'm filling out this ________.
A. For how much?
B. …………

[13–18]
A. How many ________s does the State Street Bank have?
B. …………

Do you have a bank account? What kind? Where?
Do you ever use traveler's checks? When?
Do you have a credit card? What kind? When do you use it?

[1–23, 27–79]
A. My doctor checked my **head** and said everything is okay.
B. I'm glad to hear that.

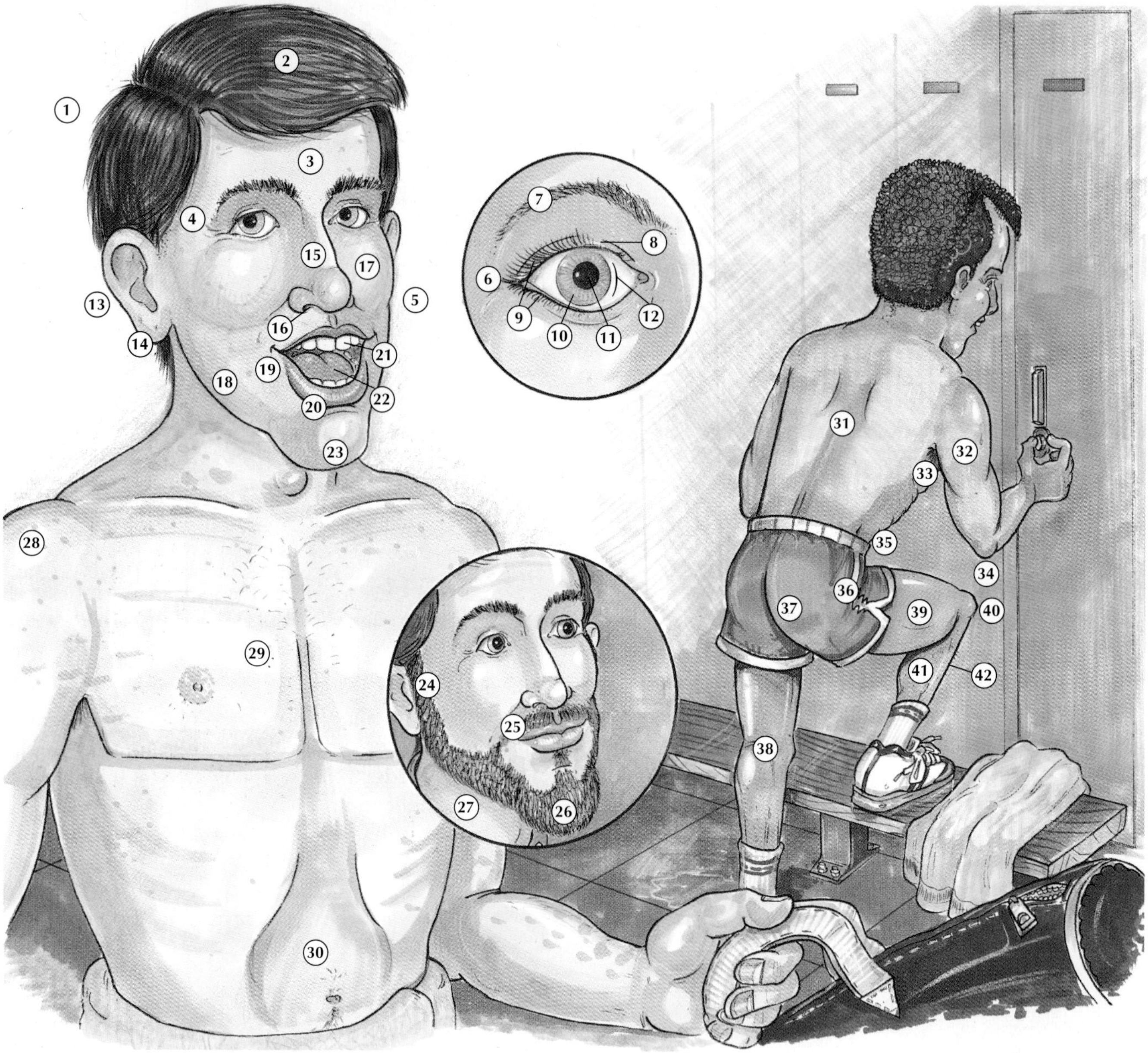

頭 **1.** head
髪 **2.** hair
額 **3.** forehead
こめかみ **4.** temple
顔 **5.** face
目 **6.** eye
まゆ **7.** eyebrow
まぶた **8.** eyelid
まつげ **9.** eyelashes
こう彩 **10.** iris
どう孔（ひとみ） **11.** pupil
角膜 **12.** cornea
耳 **13.** ear
耳たぶ **14.** earlobe

鼻 **15.** nose
鼻の穴 **16.** nostril
ほお **17.** cheek
あご **18.** jaw
口 **19.** mouth
唇 **20.** lip
歯 **21.** tooth-teeth
舌 **22.** tongue
下あご **23.** chin
もみあげ **24.** sideburn
口ひげ **25.** mustache
あごひげ **26.** beard
首 **27.** neck
肩 **28.** shoulder

胸 **29.** chest
腹 **30.** abdomen
背中 **31.** back
腕 **32.** arm
わきの下 **33.** armpit
ひじ **34.** elbow
ウエスト（胴のくびれ） **35.** waist
ヒップ（しりの側面） **36.** hip
しり（でん部） **37.** buttocks
脚 **38.** leg
太もも **39.** thigh
ひざ **40.** knee
ふくらはぎ **41.** calf
向こうずね **42.** shin

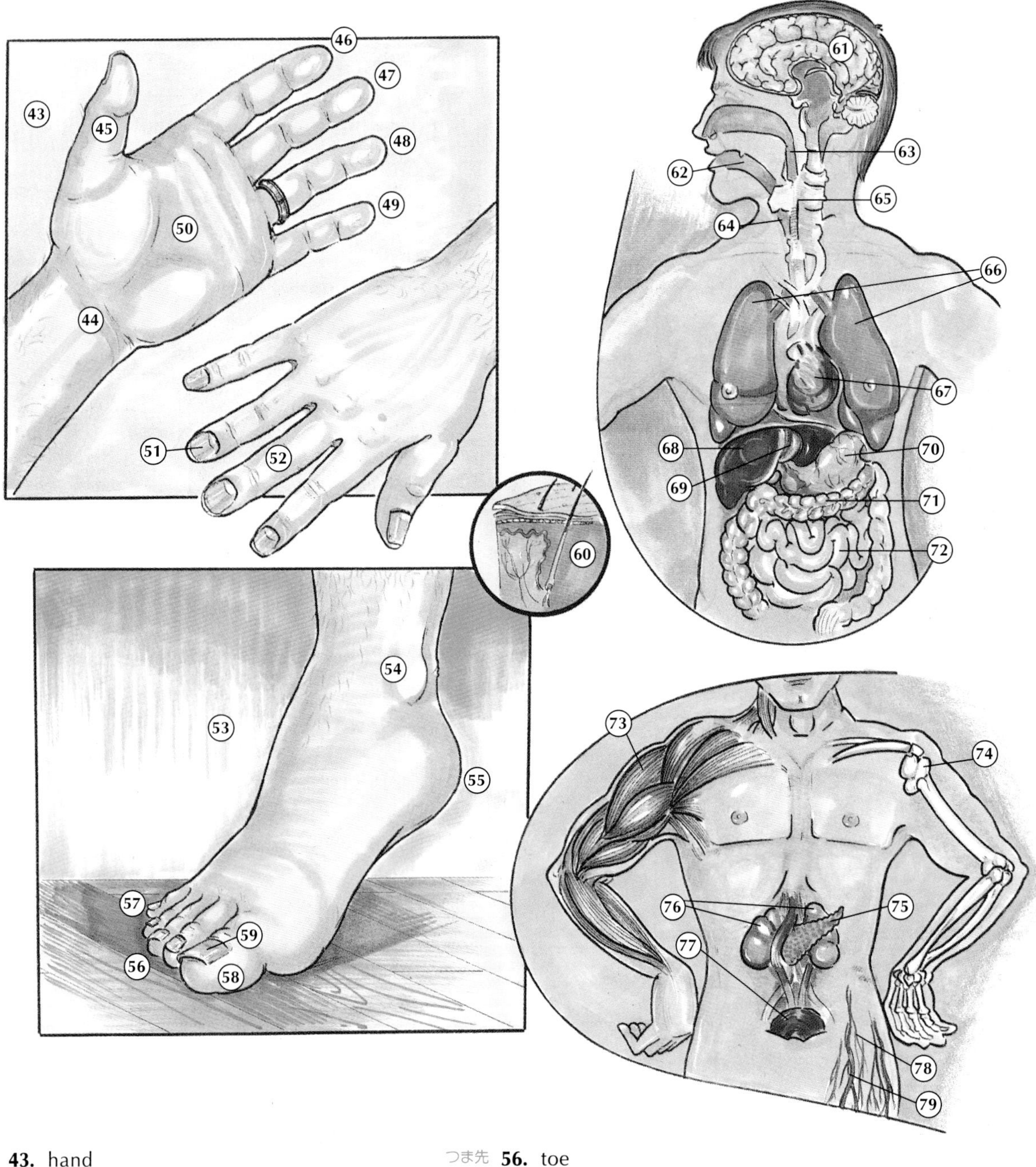

手 **43.** hand
手首 **44.** wrist
親指 **45.** thumb
人差し指 **46.** (index) finger
中指 **47.** middle finger
薬指 **48.** ring finger
小指 **49.** pinky/little finger
手のひら **50.** palm
手のつめ **51.** fingernail
指関節 **52.** knuckle
足 **53.** foot
くるぶし **54.** ankle
かかと **55.** heel

つま先 **56.** toe
足の小指 **57.** little toe
足の親指 **58.** big toe
足のつめ **59.** toenail
皮膚 **60.** skin
脳 **61.** brain
のど **62.** throat
食道 **63.** esophagus
気管 **64.** windpipe
脊髄 **65.** spinal cord
肺 **66.** lungs
心臓 **67.** heart
肝臓 **68.** liver

胆のう **69.** gallbladder
胃 **70.** stomach
大腸 **71.** large intestine
小腸 **72.** small intestine
筋肉 **73.** muscles
骨 **74.** bones
すい臓 **75.** pancreas
じん臓 **76.** kidneys
ぼうこう **77.** bladder
静脈 **78.** veins
動脈 **79.** arteries

[1, 3–8, 13–23, 27–34, 36–60]
A. Ooh!
B. What's the matter?
A. {My _______ hurts!
My _______s hurt!

[61–79]
A. My doctor wants me to have some tests.
B. Why?
A. She's concerned about my _______.

Describe yourself as completely as you can.
Which parts of the body are most important at school? at work? when you play your favorite sport?

A. What's the matter?
B. I have a/an __[1–19]__.

A. What's the matter?
B. I have __[20–26]__.

頭痛 **1.** headache
耳の痛み **2.** earache
歯痛 **3.** toothache
胃痛 **4.** stomachache
腰痛 **5.** backache
のどの痛み **6.** sore throat
熱 **7.** fever/ temperature
かぜ **8.** cold
せき **9.** cough

ウイルス **10.** virus
感染 **11.** infection
発疹 **12.** rash
虫さされ **13.** insect bite
日焼け **14.** sunburn
肩こり **15.** stiff neck
鼻水 **16.** runny nose
鼻血 **17.** bloody nose
虫歯 **18.** cavity

いぼ **19.** wart
しゃっくり **20.** (the) hiccups
寒け **21.** (the) chills
腹部の激痛（けいれん） **22.** cramps
下痢 **23.** diarrhea
胸の痛み **24.** chest pain
息切れ **25.** shortness of breath
喉こう頭炎 **26.** laryngitis

A. What's the matter?
B. { I feel [27–30] .
I'm [31–32] .
I'm [33–38] ing.

A. What's the matter?
B. { I [39–48] ed my ....
My .... is/are [49–50] .

気が遠くなる **27.** faint
めまいがする **28.** dizzy
吐き気がする **29.** nauseous
むくみがある **30.** bloated
うっ血した/充血した **31.** congested
疲労した **32.** exhausted
せきをする **33.** cough
くしゃみをする **34.** sneeze

ぜいぜい息をする **35.** wheeze
げっぷをする **36.** burp
嘔吐する **37.** vomit/throw up
出血する **38.** bleed
ひねる **39.** twist
ねんざする **40.** sprain
脱臼きゅうする **41.** dislocate
かき傷をつける **42.** scratch

すりむく **43.** scrape
あざをつける **44.** bruise
やけどする **45.** burn
骨折する **46.** break-broke
痛める **47.** hurt-hurt
切り傷をつける **48.** cut-cut
はれた **49.** swollen
かゆい **50.** itchy

A. How do you feel?
B. Not so good./Not very well./Terrible!
A. What's the matter?
B. ...., ..., and ....
A. I'm sorry to hear that.

Tell about the last time you didn't feel well. What was the matter?

Tell about a time you hurt yourself. What happened? How?

What are the symptoms of a cold? a heart problem?

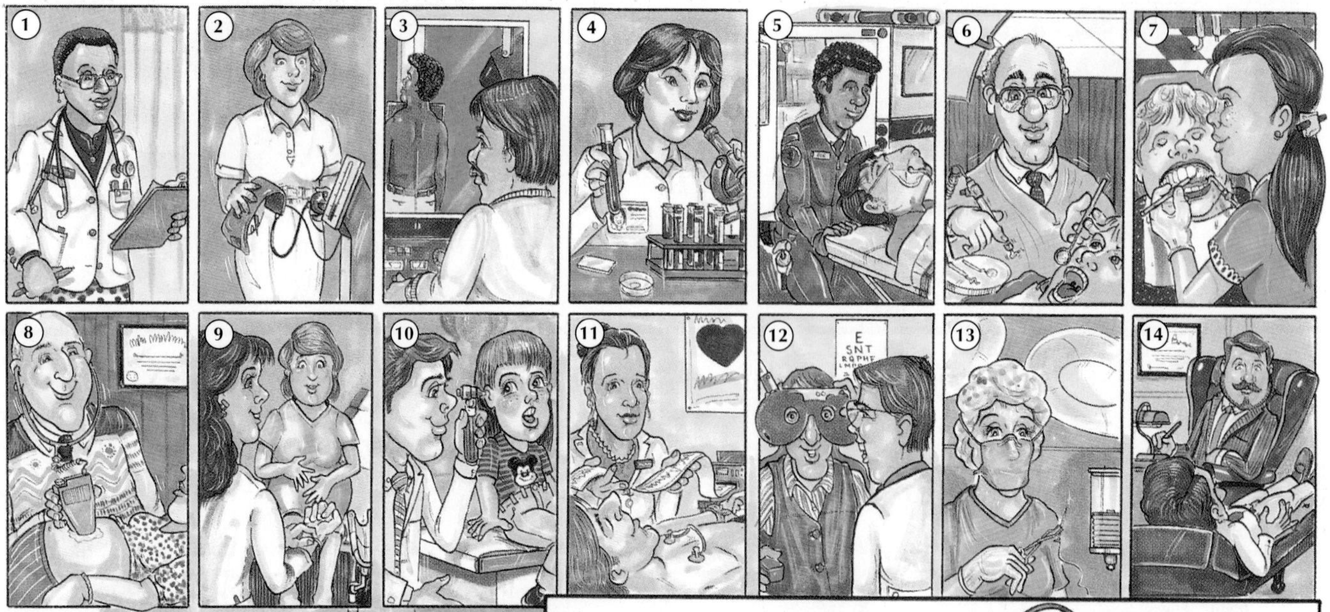

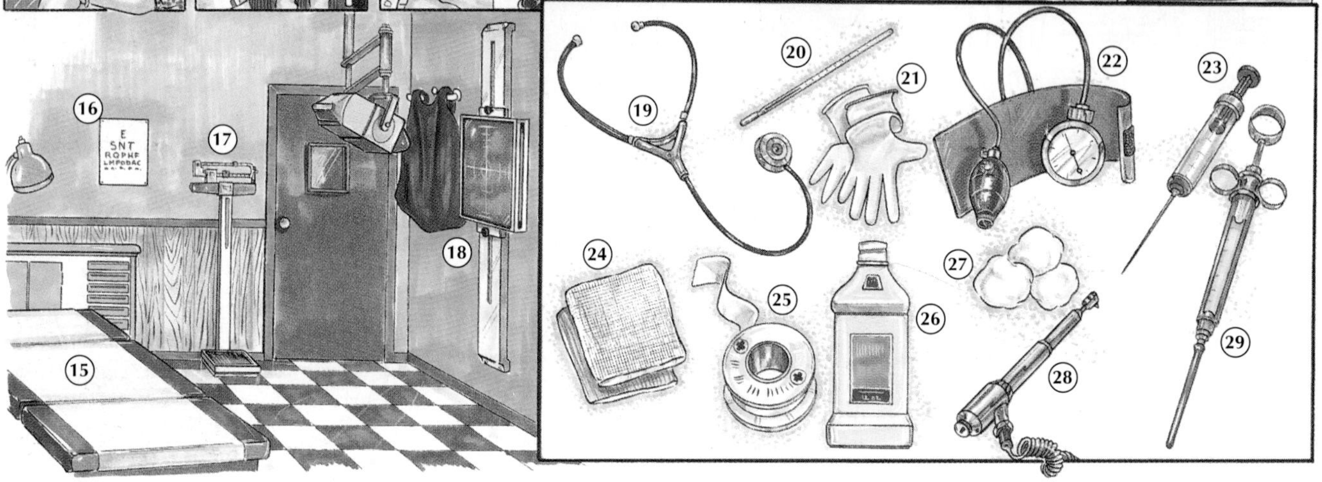

医師 **1.** doctor/physician
看護婦 **2.** nurse
レントゲン技師 **3.** X-ray technician
検査技師 **4.** lab technician
救急医療士 **5.** EMT/emergency medical technician
歯科医 **6.** dentist
口腔こう衛生士 **7.** (oral) hygienist
産科医 **8.** obstetrician
婦人科医 **9.** gynecologist
小児科医 **10.** pediatrician
心臓病専門医 **11.** cardiologist
検眼士 **12.** optometrist
外科医 **13.** surgeon
精神科医 **14.** psychiatrist
診察台 **15.** examination table
視力検査表 **16.** eye chart
体重計 **17.** scale
レントゲン写真機 **18.** X-ray machine
聴診器 **19.** stethoscope
体温計 **20.** thermometer
手袋 **21.** gloves
血圧計 **22.** blood pressure gauge
注射針/注射器 **23.** needle/syringe
ガーゼ **24.** bandages/gauze
ばんそうこう **25.** adhesive tape
アルコール **26.** alcohol
脱脂綿 **27.** cotton balls
ドリル **28.** drill
麻酔薬 **29.** anesthetic/Novocaine

[1–14]
A. What do you do?
B. I'm a/an ________.

[15–18]
A. Please step over here to the ________.
B. Okay.

[19–29]
A. Please hand me the ________.
B. Here you are.

Where do you go for medical care? How often? Who examines you? What does he/she do?

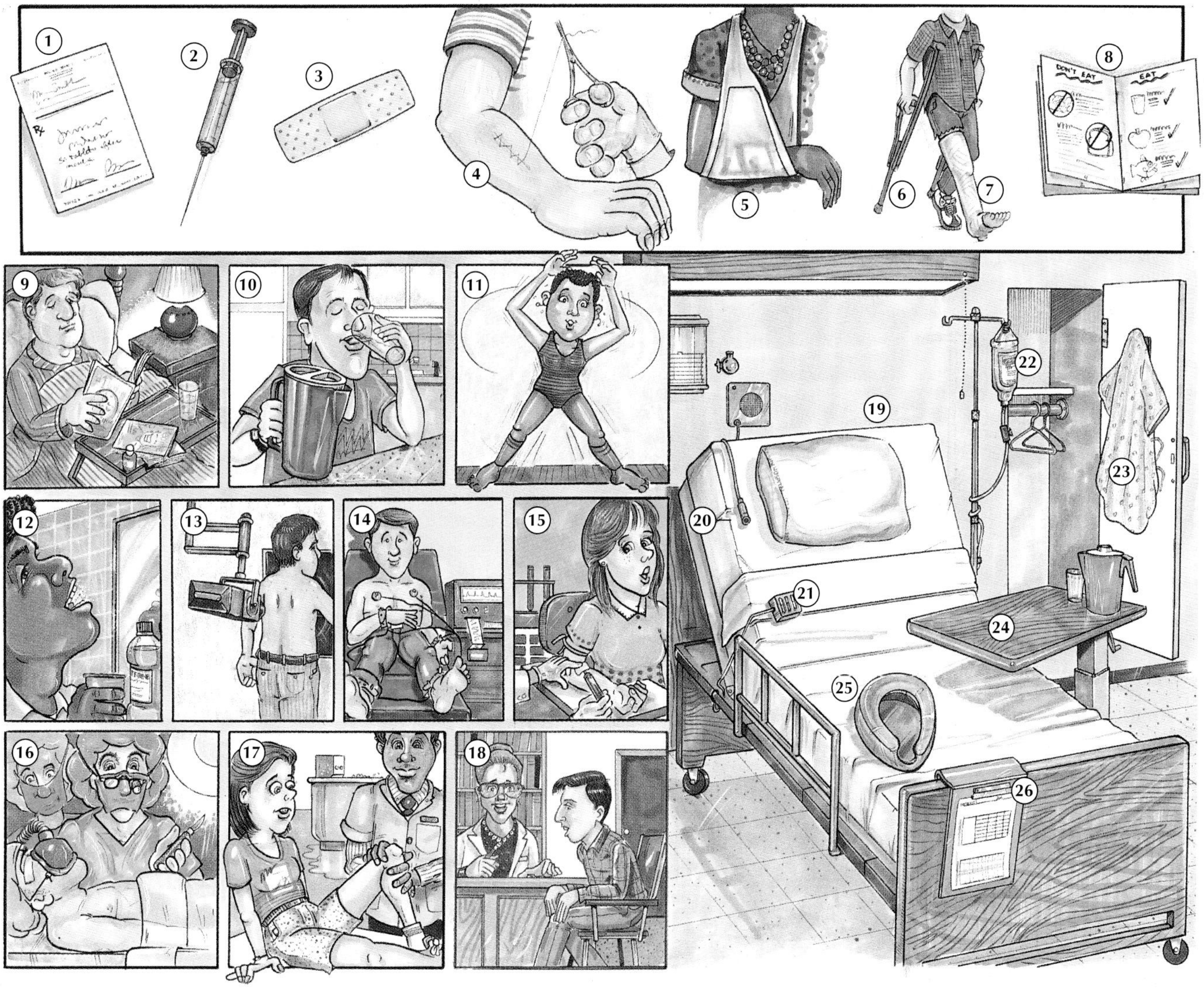

処方せん **1.** prescription	流動食をとる **10.** drink fluids	カウンセリング **18.** counseling
注射 **2.** injection/shot	からだを動かす **11.** exercise	治療用ベッド **19.** hospital bed
救急ばんそうこう **3.** bandaid	うがいをする **12.** gargle	呼出しボタン **20.** call button
縫合 **4.** stitches	レントゲン写真 **13.** X-rays	ベッド調節器 **21.** bed control
三角巾 **5.** sling	検査 **14.** tests	点滴 **22.** I.V.
松葉杖 **6.** crutches	血液検査 **15.** blood work/ blood tests	患者用ガウン **23.** hospital gown
ギプス **7.** cast	手術 **16.** surgery	(寝室用の)テーブル **24.** bed table
食餌療法 **8.** diet	理学療法 **17.** physical therapy	(病人用)便器 **25.** bed pan
安静にする **9.** rest in bed		カルテ **26.** medical chart

[1–8]
A. What did the doctor do?
B. She/He gave me (a/an) ______.

[9–18]
A. What did the doctor say?
B. { She/He told me to [9–12].
She/He told me I need [13–18].

[19–26]
A. This is your ______.
B. I see.

When did you have your last medical checkup?
What did the doctor say?

Have you ever been in the hospital?
When? Why? Tell about your experience.

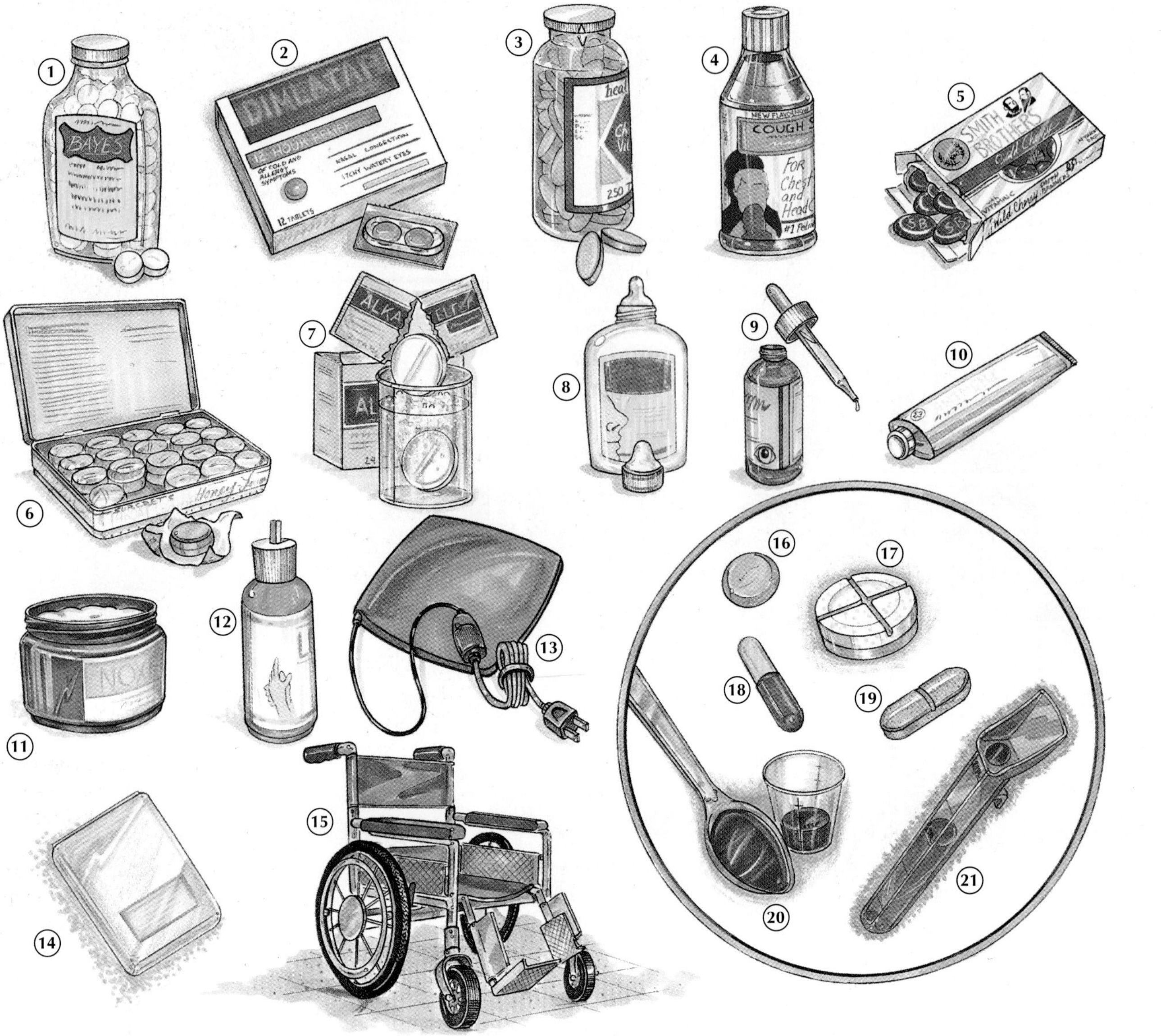

アスピリン	**1.** aspirin	鼻炎用スプレー・消炎スプレー	**8.** decongestant spray/nasal spray	車いす	**15.** wheelchair
かぜ薬	**2.** cold tablets	目薬	**9.** eye drops	丸薬	**16.** pill
ビタミン剤	**3.** vitamins	軟こう	**10.** ointment	錠剤	**17.** tablet
せき止めシロップ	**4.** cough syrup	（薬用）クリーム	**11.** creme	カプセル	**18.** capsule
せき止めドロップ	**5.** cough drops	（薬用）ローション	**12.** lotion	カプレット（カプセル型錠剤）	**19.** caplet
のどあめ	**6.** throat lozenges	ヒーティングパッド（加温器）	**13.** heating pad	ティースプーン	**20.** teaspoon
制酸剤	**7.** antacid tablets	氷のう	**14.** ice pack	テーブルスプーン	**21.** tablespoon

[1–15] A. What did the doctor say?
B. She/He told me to take [1–4].
She/He told me to use (a/an) [5–15].

[16–21] A. What's the dosage?
B. One ______, every three hours.

What medicines do you take or use?
For what ailments?

Describe any medical treatments or medicines in your country that are different from the ones in these lessons.

THE POST OFFICE［郵便局］

手紙	**1.**	letter
はがき	**2.**	postcard
航空郵便/航空書簡	**3.**	air letter/ aerogramme
小包	**4.**	package/parcel
第一種（封書）	**5.**	first class
航空便	**6.**	air mail
郵便小包	**7.**	parcel post
書籍小包/第三種	**8.**	book rate/ third class
書留	**9.**	registered mail
速達	**10.**	express mail/ overnight mail
切手	**11.**	stamp
切手シート	**12.**	sheet of stamps
巻いてある切手/巻き切手	**13.**	roll of stamps
切手帳	**14.**	book of stamps
郵便為替	**15.**	money order
転居届	**16.**	change-of-address form
選抜徴兵登録用紙	**17.**	selective service registration form
封筒	**18.**	envelope
あて先	**19.**	address
郵便番号	**20.**	zip code
差出人住所氏名	**21.**	return address
切手・郵便料金	**22.**	stamp/postage
消印	**23.**	postmark
投函口	**24.**	mail slot
窓口	**25.**	window
郵便局員	**26.**	postal worker/ postal clerk
はかり	**27.**	scale
切手自動販売機	**28.**	stamp machine
郵便車	**29.**	mail truck
郵便ポスト	**30.**	mailbox
郵便配達人	**31.**	letter carrier/ mail carrier
郵便袋	**32.**	mail bag

[1–4]
A. Where are you going?
B. To the post office.

[5–10]
A. How do you want to send it?

[11–17]
A. Next!
B. I'd like a ______, please.

[19–22]
A. Do you want me to mail this letter for you?
B. Yes, thanks.
A. Oops! You forgot the ______!

What time does your letter carrier deliver your mail? Does he/she drive a mail truck or carry a mail bag and walk?

Describe the post office you use:
How many postal windows are there?
Is there a stamp machine?
Are the postal workers friendly?

Tell about the postal system in your country.

図書館員/司書 **1.** librarian
貸出カウンター **2.** checkout desk
図書館補助員 **3.** library assistant
マイクロフィルム **4.** microfilm
マイクロフィッシュ **5.** microfiche
カード目録 **6.** card catalog
オンライン目録 **7.** online catalog
書棚 **8.** shelves
案内カウンター **9.** information desk
コピー機 **10.** copier/(photo) copy machine

参考図書案内員 **11.** reference librarian
参考図書室 **12.** reference section
地図帳 **13.** atlas
百科事典 **14.** encyclopedia
辞書 **15.** dictionary
視聴覚コーナー **16.** media section
ビデオ **17.** videotape
レコード **18.** record
テープ **19.** tape
コンピューターディスク **20.** computer diskette
定期刊行物コーナー **21.** periodicals section

新聞 **22.** newspaper
雑誌 **23.** magazine
定期刊行物/専門雑誌 **24.** journal
検索カード **25.** call card
分類番号 **26.** call number
著者名 **27.** author
書名 **28.** title
事項 **29.** subject
貸出カード **30.** library card

[1–11]
A. Excuse me. Where's/ Where are the ______?
B. Over there, at/near/next to the ______.

[12–24]
A. Excuse me. Where can I find (a/an) [13–15, 17–20, 22–24]?
B. Look in the [12, 16, 21] over there.

[27–29]
A. May I help you?
B. Yes, please. I'm having trouble finding a book.
A. Do you know the ______?
B. Yes. …………

Do you go to a library? Which one? What does this library have? Describe how you use the library.

事務室 **1.** office
保健室 **2.** nurse's office
学生指導室 **3.** guidance office
食堂 **4.** cafeteria
校長室 **5.** principal's office
教室 **6.** classroom
ロッカー **7.** locker
語学実習室 **8.** language lab
化学実験室 **9.** chemistry lab

教職員室 **10.** teachers' lounge
体育館 **11.** gym/gymnasium
更衣室 **12.** locker room
講堂 **13.** auditorium
グラウンド **14.** field
（屋外）観覧席 **15.** bleachers
競技用トラック **16.** track
校長 **17.** principal
教頭 **18.** assistant principal

保健婦/養護の先生 **19.** (school) nurse
学生指導員 **20.** guidance counselor
学食監視員 **21.** lunchroom monitor
食堂従業員 **22.** cafeteria worker
自動車運転教習指導員 **23.** driver's ed instructor
教師 **24.** teacher
コーチ **25.** coach
用務員 **26.** custodian

[1–16] A. Where are you going?
B. I'm going to the ________.*
A. Do you have a hall pass?
B. Yes. Here it is.

With 6 and 7, use: I'm going to my ________.

[17–26] A. Who's that?
B. That's the new ________.

Describe the school where you study English. Tell about the rooms, offices, and people.

Tell about differences between schools in the United States and in your country.

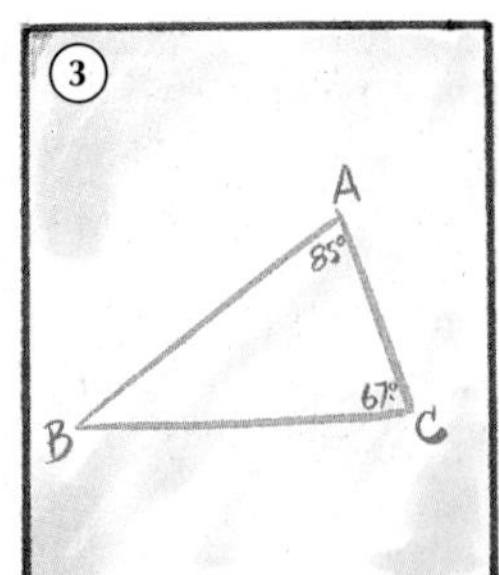

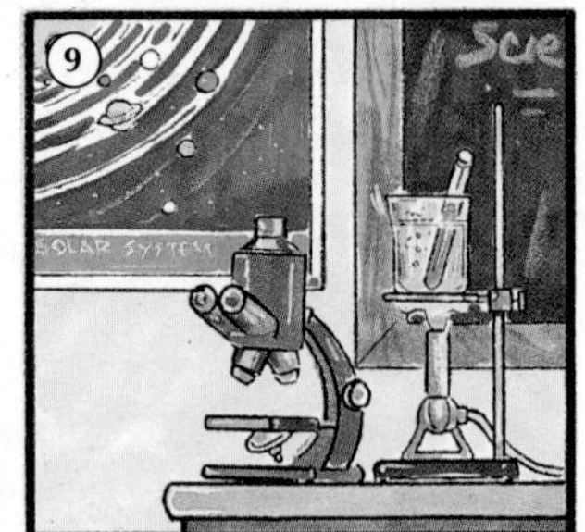

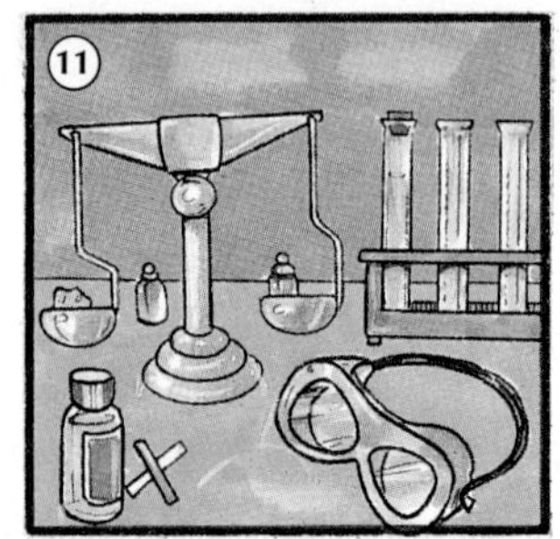

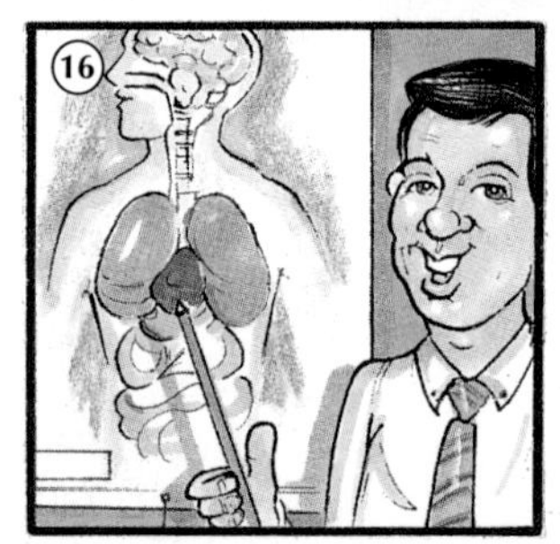

数学 **1.** math/mathematics
代数 **2.** algebra
幾何 **3.** geometry
三角法 **4.** trigonometry
微分・積分（計算法） **5.** calculus
英語 **6.** English
歴史 **7.** history
地理 **8.** geography

科学 **9.** science
生物 **10.** biology
化学 **11.** chemistry
物理 **12.** physics
スペイン語 **13.** Spanish
フランス語 **14.** French
家庭科 **15.** home economics
保健 **16.** health

工芸 **17.** industrial arts/shop
自動車運転教習 **18.** driver's education/driver's ed
タイプ **19.** typing
美術 **20.** art
音楽 **21.** music

バンド/楽隊 **22.** band
オーケストラ **23.** orchestra
合唱団 **24.** choir/chorus

演劇 **25.** drama
(アメリカン)フットボール **26.** football
校内新聞 **27.** school newspaper

卒業記念アルバム **28.** yearbook
文芸誌 **29.** literary magazine
生徒会 **30.** student government

[1–21]
A. What do you have next period?
B. ________. How about you?
A. ________.
B. There's the bell. I've got to go.

[22–30]
A. Are you going home right after school?
B. { No. I have [22–26] practice.
No. I have a [27–30] meeting.

What is/was your favorite subject? Why? What extracurricular activities do/did you participate in?

A. What do you do?
B. I'm an **accountant**. How about you?
A. I'm a **carpenter**.

会計士 **1.** accountant
俳優/男優 **2.** actor
女優 **3.** actress
建築家 **4.** architect
画家 **5.** artist

組立工 **6.** assembler
パン屋 **7.** baker
床屋 **8.** barber
簿記係 **9.** bookkeeper
石工 **10.** bricklayer/mason

バス運転手 **11.** bus driver
肉屋 **12.** butcher
大工 **13.** carpenter
レジ係 **14.** cashier
コック **15.** chef/cook

コンピューター・プログラマー **16.** computer programmer
建設作業員 **17.** construction worker
（国際）宅配便/メッセンジャー配達便 **18.** courier/messenger
用務員 **19.** custodian/janitor
データ処理員 **20.** data processor
配達員 **21.** delivery person
電気工 **22.** electrician
農夫 **23.** farmer
消防士 **24.** firefighter
漁師 **25.** fisherman
作業長 **26.** foreman
庭師 **27.** gardener
美容師 **28.** hairdresser
家政婦 **29.** housekeeper
記者 **30.** journalist/reporter

[At a job interview]
A. Are you an experienced ________?
B. Yes. I'm a very experienced ________.

A. How long have you been a/an ________?
B. I've been a/an ________ for .... months/years.

Which of these occupations do you think are the most interesting? the most difficult? Why?

A. What's your occupation?
B. I'm a **lawyer**.
A. A **lawyer**?
B. Yes. That's right.

弁護士 **1.** lawyer
機械整備工 **2.** mechanic
モデル **3.** model
ニュースキャスター **4.** newscaster
ペンキ屋 **5.** painter
薬剤師 **6.** pharmacist
写真家 **7.** photographer
パイロット **8.** pilot
配管工 **9.** plumber
警官 **10.** police officer
不動産業者 **11.** real estate agent
受付係 **12.** receptionist
修繕屋 **13.** repairperson
販売員 **14.** salesperson
清掃課員 **15.** sanitation worker

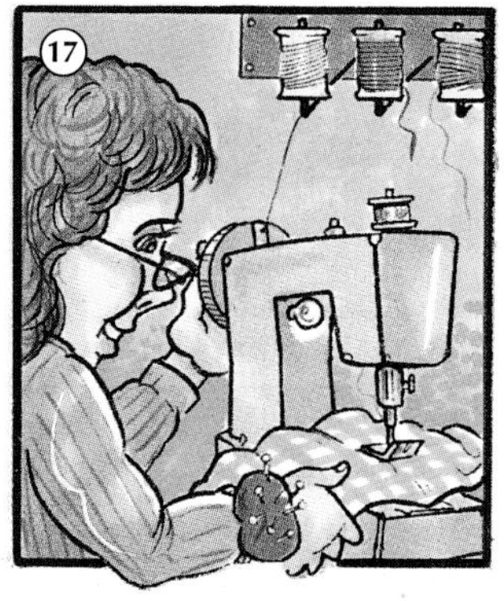

科学者 **16.** scientist
裁縫師（お針子） **17.** seamstress
秘書 **18.** secretary
警備員 **19.** security guard
倉庫係 **20.** stock clerk

仕立屋 **21.** tailor
タクシー運転手 **22.** taxi driver
教師 **23.** teacher
翻訳者/通訳者 **24.** translator/interpreter
旅行代理業者 **25.** travel agent

トラック運転手 **26.** truck driver
ウエイター **27.** waiter
ウエイトレス **28.** waitress
溶接工 **29.** welder
獣医 **30.** veterinarian

A. Are you still a ________?
B. No. I'm a ________.
A. Oh. That's interesting.

A. What kind of job would you like in the future?
B. I'd like to be a ________.

Do you work? What's your occupation?
What are the occupations of people in your family?

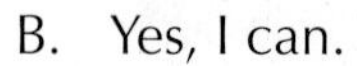

A. Can you **act**?
B. Yes, I can.

演技する **1.** act
部品を組み立てる **2.** assemble *components*
焼く **3.** bake
ものを組み立てる/ **4.** build *things*
ものを建造する construct *things*
掃除する **5.** clean
料理する **6.** cook
ピザを配達する **7.** deliver *pizzas*
建物を設計する **8.** design *buildings*
絵をかく **9.** draw
トラックを運転する **10.** drive a *truck*
ファイルする **11.** file
飛行機を操縦する **12.** fly *an airplane*
野菜を育てる **13.** grow *vegetables*
ビルを警備する **14.** guard *buildings*

芝を刈る **15.** mow *lawns*
装置を操作する **16.** operate *equipment*
ペンキを塗る **17.** paint
ピアノを弾く **18.** play the *piano*
修繕する **19.** repair *things*/fix *things*

車を販売する **20.** sell *cars*
食事を給仕する **21.** serve *food*
縫う **22.** sew
歌う **23.** sing
教える **24.** teach

訳す **25.** translate
タイプを打つ **26.** type
食器を洗う **27.** wash *dishes*
文章を書く **28.** write

A. What do you do for a living?
B. I ________.

A. Do you know how to ________?
B. Yes. I've been ________ing for years.

Tell about your work abilities.
What can you do?

受付 **1.** reception area
コート掛け **2.** coat rack
クローゼット **3.** coat closet
連絡板 **4.** message board
郵便箱 **5.** mailbox
書類キャビネット **6.** file cabinet
事務用品入れ **7.** supply cabinet
保管品戸棚 **8.** storage cabinet
ワークステーション/仕事場 **9.** workstation
コンピューター作業場 **10.** computer workstation
冷水器/ウォータークーラー **11.** water cooler
コーヒーワゴン **12.** coffee cart

オフィス（執務室） **13.** office
メールルーム **14.** mailroom
郵便料金メーター **15.** postage machine/postage meter
コピー機 **16.** copier/(photo) copy machine
くず入れ **17.** waste receptacle
備品置場 **18.** supply room
倉庫 **19.** storage room
会議室 **20.** conference room
会議用テーブル **21.** conference table
ホワイトボード **22.** whiteboard/dry erase board
休憩室 **23.** employee lounge

コーヒーメーカー **24.** coffee machine
清涼飲料水自動販売機 **25.** soda machine
受付係 **26.** receptionist
タイピスト **27.** typist
書類整理係 **28.** file clerk
秘書 **29.** secretary
総務アシスタント **30.** administrative assistant
総務課長 **31.** office manager
事務アシスタント **32.** office assistant
雇用主/社長 **33.** employer/boss

[1–25] A. Where's ....?
B. { He's/She's in the/his/her ________.*
He's/She's at the/his/her ________.†

*1, 13, 14, 18–20, 23 †2–12, 15–17, 21, 22, 24, 25

[26–33] A. Who's he/she?
B. He's/She's the new ________.

Describe an office you are familiar with. Tell about the rooms, the work areas, and the employees.

A. Do you know how to work this **computer**?
B. No, I don't.
A. Let me show you how.

コンピューター **1.** computer
ビデオ端末 **2.** VDT/video display terminal
ドットプリンター **3.** (dot-matrix) printer
高品質プリンター **4.** (letter-quality) printer
レーザープリンター **5.** (laser) printer
ワープロ **6.** word processor
タイプライター **7.** typewriter
電卓 **8.** calculator
計算器 **9.** adding machine
小型録音機 **10.** microcassette recorder/dictaphone
電話機 **11.** telephone
ヘッドホン **12.** headset
システムホーン **13.** phone system
テレックス **14.** telex machine
ファクシミリ **15.** fax machine
鉛筆削り **16.** pencil sharpener
電気鉛筆削り **17.** electric pencil sharpener
紙断裁機/押し切り **18.** paper cutter
プラスティックリング製本機 **19.** plastic binding machine
郵便ばかり **20.** postal scale
シュレッダー（書類断裁機） **21.** paper shredder

A. I think this _______ is broken!
B. I'll take a look at it.

A. Have you seen the new _______?
B. No, I haven't.
A. It's much better than the old one!

Do you know how to operate a computer? a fax machine? Give step-by-step instructions for using some type of office equipment.

OFFICE FURNISHINGS [事務備品]

机 **1.** desk
回転いす **2.** swivel chair
ローロデックス（回転式インデックスファイル） **3.** rolodex
鉛筆立て **4.** pencil cup
レタートレー **5.** letter tray/stacking tray
メモホルダー **6.** memo holder
卓上カレンダー **7.** desk calendar
卓上スタンド **8.** desk lamp
名札 **9.** nameplate
デスクマット **10.** desk pad
くず入れ **11.** wastebasket

事務用いす **12.** posture chair/clerical chair
カレンダー **13.** wall calendar
計画表 **14.** wall planner
書類キャビネット **15.** file cabinet
ホッチキス **16.** stapler
針はがし（リムーバー） **17.** staple remover
セロテープ台 **18.** tape dispenser
クリップ入れ **19.** paper clip dispenser
名刺 **20.** business cards
クリップボード **21.** clipboard
手帳 **22.** appointment book
システム手帳 **23.** organizer/personal planner

出勤簿 **24.** timesheet
給料支払い小切手 **25.** paycheck
ペーパーナイフ **26.** letter opener
はさみ **27.** scissors
パンチ **28.** punch
三穴パンチ **29.** 3-hole punch
スタンプ台 **30.** stamp pad/ink pad
ゴム印 **31.** rubber stamp
ペン **32.** pen
鉛筆 **33.** pencil
シャープペンシル **34.** mechanical pencil
蛍光ペン/ラインマーカー **35.** highlighter (pen)
消しゴム **36.** eraser

[1–15]
A. Welcome to the company.
B. Thank you.
A. How do you like your ________?
B. It's/They're very nice.

[16–36]
A. My desk is such a mess! I can't find my ________!
B. Here it is/Here they are next to your ________.

Which items on this page do you have? Do you have an appointment book, personal planner, or calendar? How do you remember important things such as appointments, meetings, and birthdays?

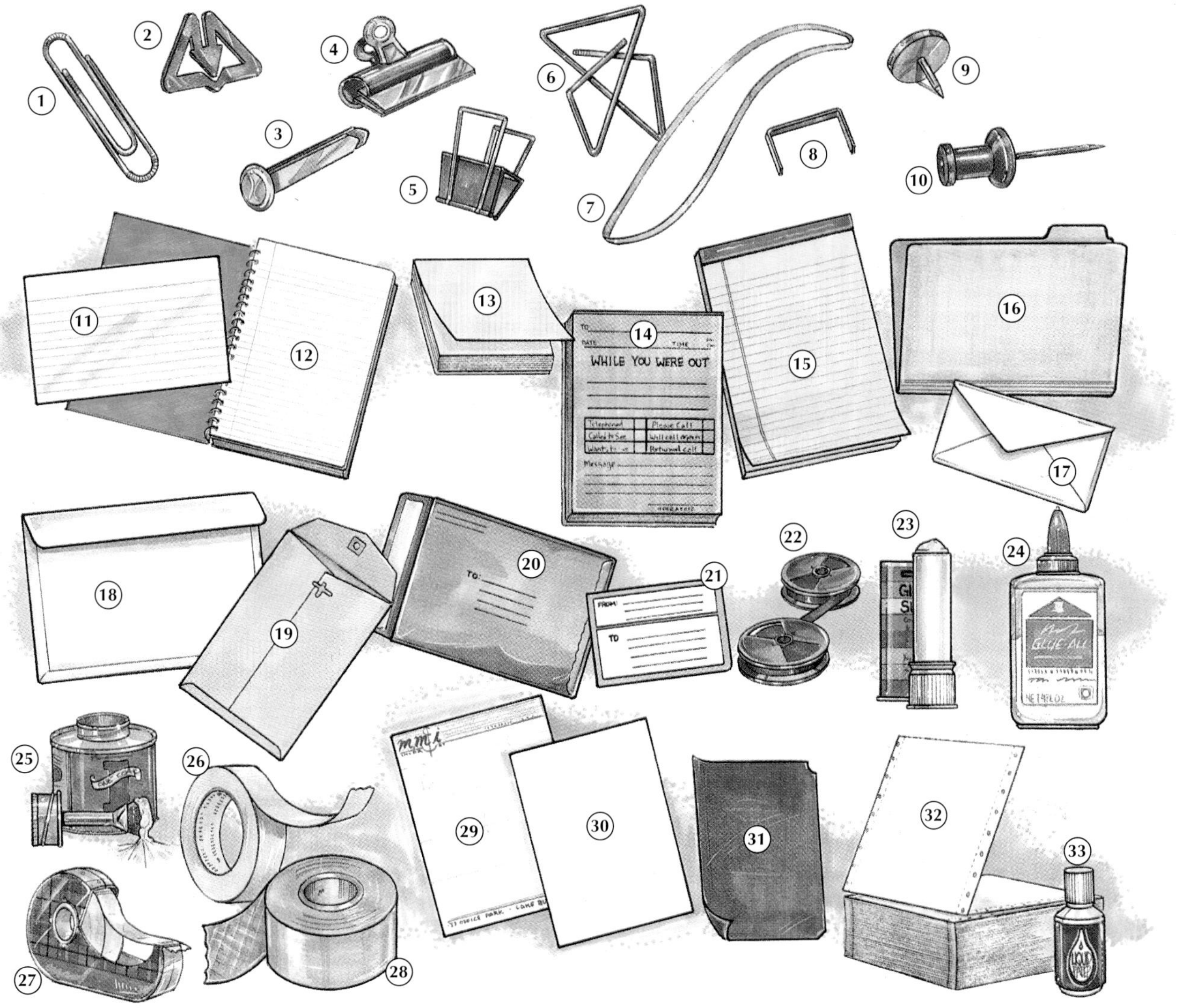

クリップ **1.** paper clip
プラスチッククリップ **2.** plastic clip
割びょう **3.** paper fastener
目玉クリップ **4.** bulldog clip
ダブルクリップ **5.** binder clip
留め金 **6.** clamp
輪ゴム **7.** rubber band
ホッチキス針 **8.** staple
画びょう **9.** thumbtack
画びょう/ピン **10.** pushpin
索引カード **11.** index card
メモ用紙 **12.** memo pad/ note pad

(商標名)ポスト・イット/符箋紙 **13.** Post-It note pad
伝言用紙 **14.** message pad
リーガルパッド (8.5×14インチの用紙) **15.** legal pad
フォルダー **16.** file folder/ manila folder
封筒 **17.** envelope
大型封筒 **18.** catalog envelope
留め金付封筒 **19.** clasp envelope
郵便封筒 **20.** mailer
宛名（用）ラベル **21.** mailing label
タイプライターリボン **22.** typewriter ribbon
スティックのり **23.** gluestick

接着剤 **24.** glue
ゴムのり **25.** rubber cement
マスキングテープ **26.** masking tape
セロテープ **27.** Scotch tape/ cellophane tape
ガムテープ **28.** sealing tape/ package mailing tape
便せん **29.** stationery
タイプ用紙 **30.** typing paper
カーボン紙 **31.** carbon paper
コンピューター用紙 **32.** computer paper
修正液 **33.** correction fluid

A. { We've run out of [1–23] s.
We've run out of [24–33] .
B. I'll get some more from the supply room.

A. Could I borrow a/an/some [1–33] ?
B. Sure. Here you are.

Which supplies do you use? What do you use them for? Where do you buy them?

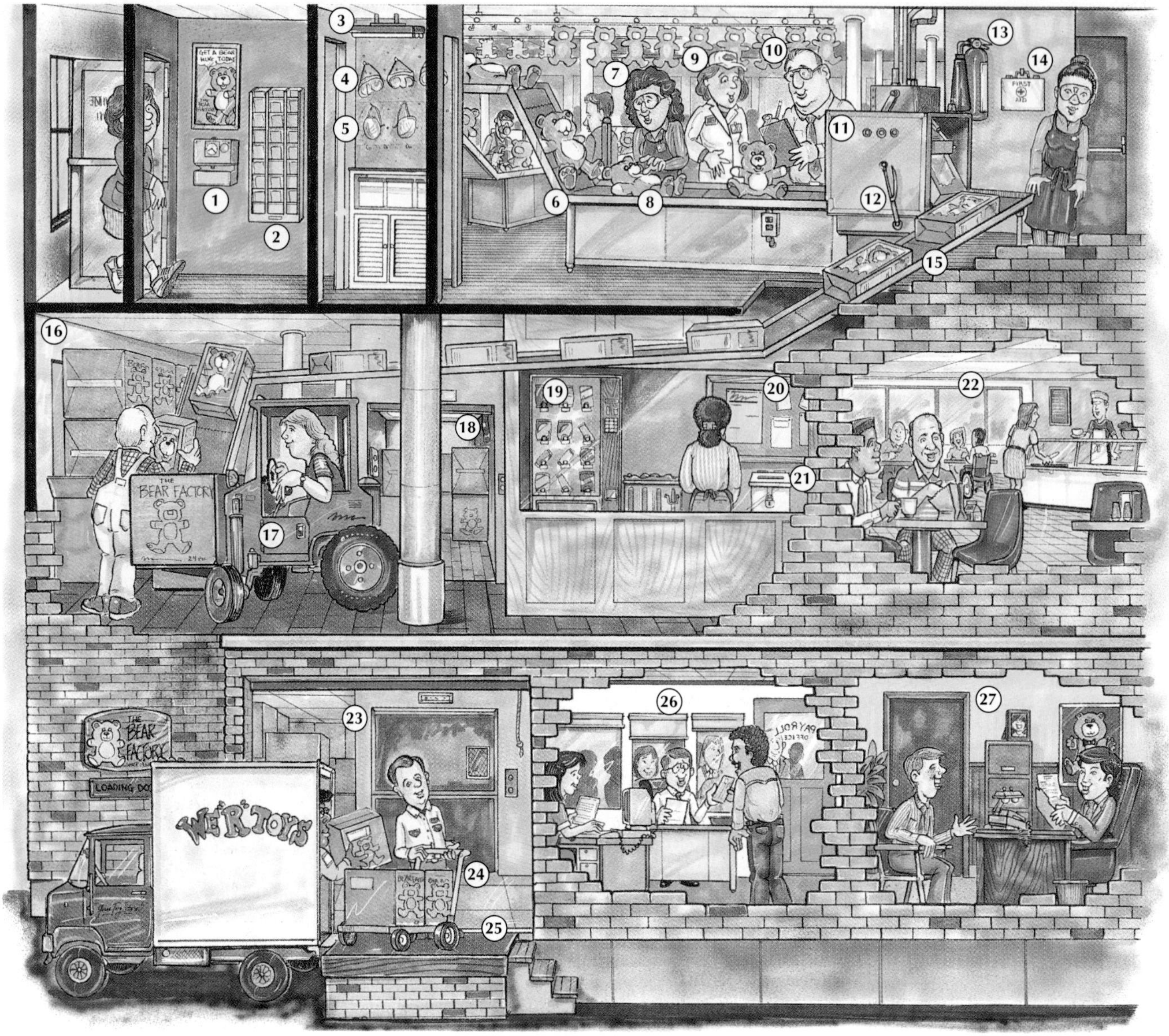

タイムレコーダー **1.** time clock
タイムカード **2.** time cards
備品置き場 **3.** supply room
安全めがね **4.** safety glasses
（安全）マスク **5.** masks
組み立てライン **6.** (assembly) line
工員 **7.** worker
作業場 **8.** work station
品質管理監督 **9.** quality control supervisor

作業長 **10.** foreman
機械 **11.** machine
レバー（てこ） **12.** lever
消火器 **13.** fire extinguisher
救急箱 **14.** first-aid kit
ベルトコンベアー **15.** conveyor belt
倉庫 **16.** warehouse
フォークリフト **17.** forklift
荷物用エレベーター **18.** freight elevator
自動販売機 **19.** vending machine

組合掲示板 **20.** union notice
投書箱 **21.** suggestion box
食堂 **22.** cafeteria
発送部 **23.** shipping department
台車 **24.** hand truck
荷積み台 **25.** loading dock
給与課（部） **26.** payroll office
人事課（部） **27.** personnel office

A. Excuse me. I'm a new employee. Where's/Where are the ________?
B. Next to/Near/In/On the ________.

A. Have you seen *Fred*?
B. Yes. He's in/on/at/next to/near the ________.

Are there any factories where you live? What kind? What are the working conditions there?

What products do factories in your country produce?

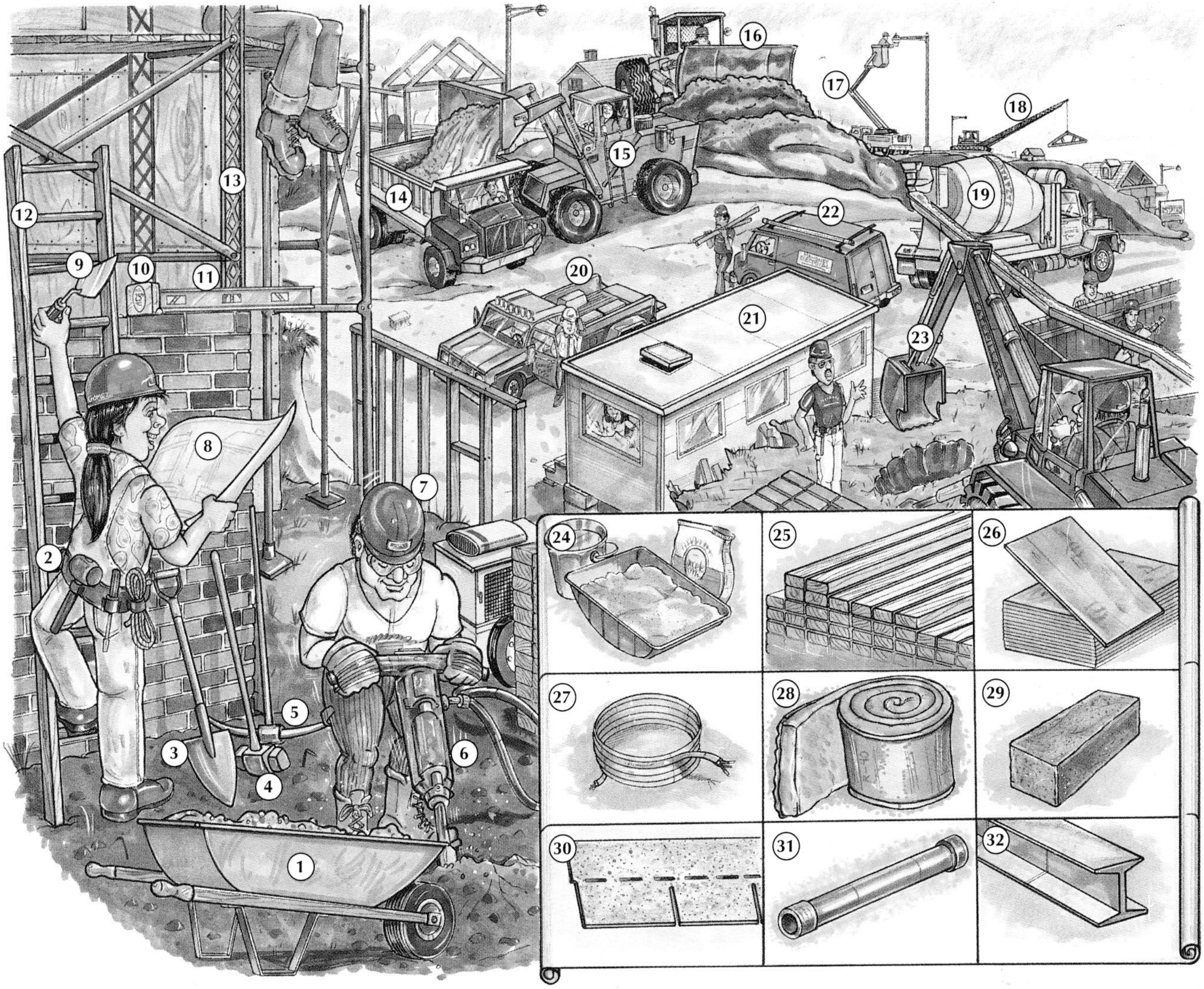

手押し車 **1.** wheelbarrow
工具ベルト **2.** toolbelt
スコップ **3.** shovel
大ハンマー **4.** sledgehammer
つるはし **5.** pickax
削岩ドリル **6.** jackhammer/pneumatic drill
ヘルメット **7.** helmet/hard hat
青写真 **8.** blueprints
こて **9.** trowel
巻き尺 **10.** tape measure

水準器 **11.** level
はしご **12.** ladder
足場 **13.** scaffolding
ダンプカー **14.** dump truck
シャベルローダー **15.** front-end loader
ブルドーザー **16.** bulldozer
高所作業用クレーン **17.** cherry picker
クレーン車 **18.** crane
コンクリートミキサー車 **19.** cement mixer
小型トラック **20.** pickup truck
トレーラー **21.** trailer

ワゴン車 **22.** van
ショベルカー **23.** backhoe
セメント **24.** cement
木材 **25.** wood/lumber
ベニヤ板 **26.** plywood
針金 **27.** wire
絶縁材 **28.** insulation
れんが **29.** brick
こけら板 **30.** shingle
導管 **31.** pipe
梁 **32.** girder/beam

[1–12]
A. Could you get me that/those ______?
B. Sure.

[13–23]
A. Watch out for that ______!
B. Oh! Thanks for the warning!

[24–32]
A. Are we going to have enough [24–28] / [29–32] s to finish the job?
B. I think so.

What building materials is your home made of?

Tell about a construction site near your home or school.

ヘッドライト **1.** headlight
バンパー **2.** bumper
方向指示灯/ウインカー **3.** turn signal
駐車灯 **4.** parking light
タイヤ **5.** tire
ホイールキャップ **6.** hubcap
ボンネット **7.** hood
フロントガラス **8.** windshield
ワイパー **9.** windshield wipers
サイドミラー **10.** side mirror
アンテナ **11.** antenna
サンルーフ **12.** sunroof
キャリア **13.** luggage rack/ luggage carrier
リヤガラス **14.** rear windshield
（後部ガラス用）デフロスター **15.** rear defroster
トランク **16.** trunk
テールランプ **17.** taillight
ブレーキランプ **18.** brake light
バックライト **19.** backup light
ナンバープレート **20.** license plate
排気管 **21.** tailpipe
マフラー **22.** muffler
トランスミッション（変速機） **23.** transmission
ガソリンタンク **24.** gas tank
ジャッキ **25.** jack
スペアタイヤ **26.** spare tire
照明筒 **27.** flare
（バッテリー充電用）ブースターケーブル **28.** jumper cables
エンジン **29.** engine
点火プラグ **30.** spark plugs
キャブレター **31.** carburetor
エアーフィルター **32.** air filter
バッテリー **33.** battery
オイルレベルゲージ **34.** dipstick
発電機 **35.** alternator
ラジエーター **36.** radiator
ファンベルト **37.** fan belt
ラジエーターホース **38.** radiator hose
ガソリンスタンド **39.** gas station/ service station
空気ポンプ **40.** air pump
整備場 **41.** service bay
整備工 **42.** mechanic
店員 **43.** attendant
ガソリンポンプ **44.** gas pump
ノズル **45.** nozzle

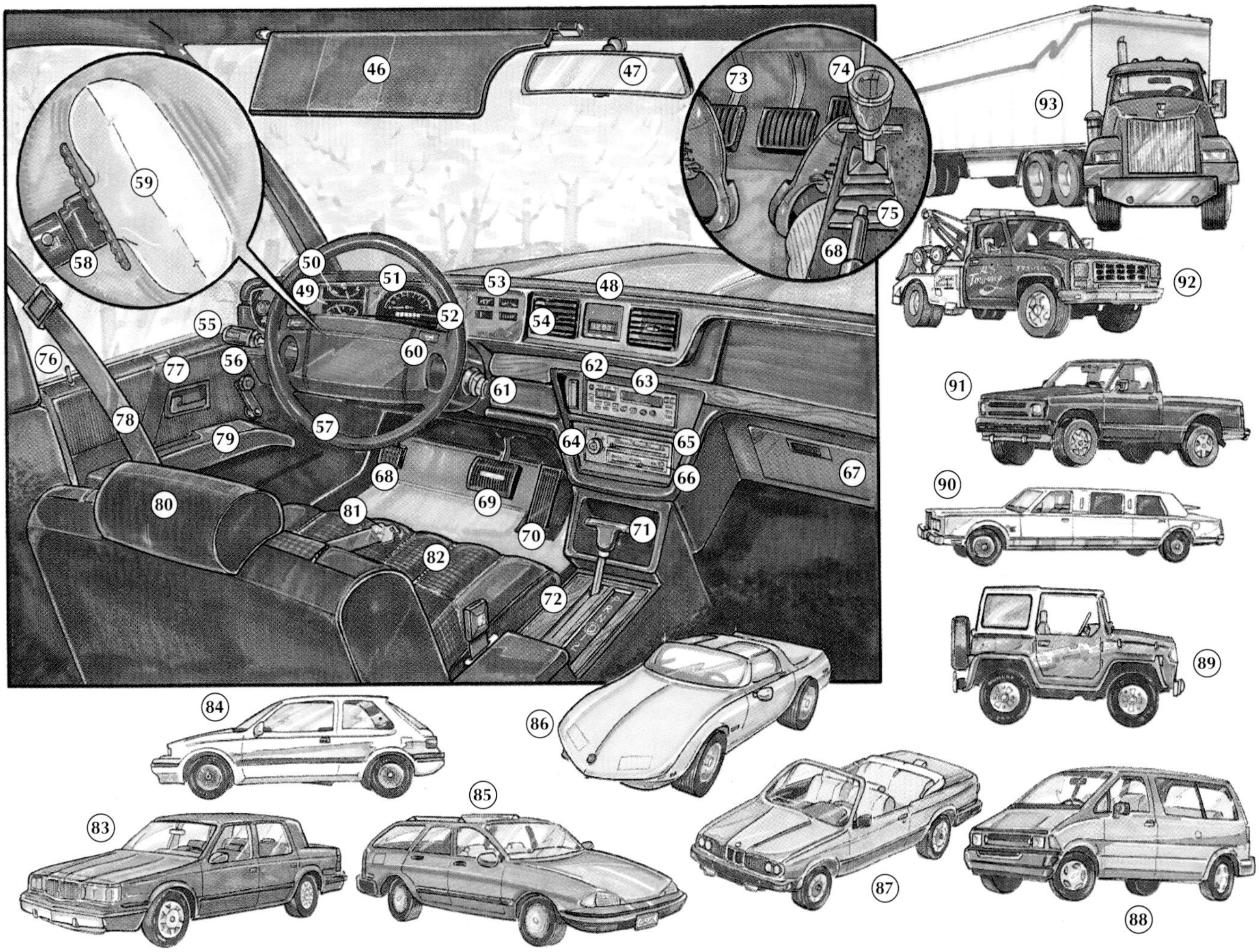

日よけ **46.** visor
バックミラー **47.** rearview mirror
ダッシュボード/計器パネル **48.** dashboard/instrument panel
ガソリンメーター **49.** gas gauge/fuel gauge
水温計 **50.** temperature gauge
スピードメーター **51.** speedometer
オドメーター(走行距離計) **52.** odometer
警告灯 **53.** warning lights
通気孔 **54.** vent
ウインカーレバー **55.** turn signal
クルーズコントロール **56.** cruise control
ハンドル **57.** steering wheel
ハンドルシャフト **58.** steering column
エアバッグ **59.** air bag
クラクション **60.** horn
イグニッション（点火スイッチ） **61.** ignition

ラジオ **62.** radio
テープデッキ **63.** tape deck/cassette player
エアコン **64.** air conditioning
ヒーター **65.** heater
デフロスター **66.** defroster
小物入れ **67.** glove compartment
サイドブレーキ **68.** emergency brake
ブレーキペダル **69.** brake
アクセルペダル **70.** accelerator/gas pedal
セレクトレバー **71.** gearshift
自動変速機(オートマチックトランスミッション) **72.** automatic transmission
クラッチペダル **73.** clutch
シフトレバー **74.** stickshift
手動変速機(マニュアルトランスミッション) **75.** manual transmission

ドアロック **76.** door lock
ドア取っ手 **77.** door handle
肩ベルト **78.** shoulder harness
ひじ掛け **79.** armrest
ヘッドレスト（安全枕） **80.** headrest
シートベルト **81.** seatbelt
座席（シート） **82.** seat
セダン（普通乗用車） **83.** sedan
ハッチバック **84.** hatchback
ライトバン **85.** station wagon
スポーツカー **86.** sports car
コンバーチブル **87.** convertible
ミニワゴン車 **88.** minivan
ジープ **89.** jeep
リムジン **90.** limousine
小型トラック **91.** pick-up truck
レッカー車 **92.** tow truck
トラック **93.** truck

[1, 3, 8–15, 23, 34–38, 46–82]
A. What's the matter with your car?
B. The ________(s) is/are broken.

[1, 4–6, 9–11, 30–33, 37, 38]
A. Can I help you?
B. Yes. I need to replace a/the ________(s).

[1, 2, 4–8, 10–14, 16–20]
A. I was just in a car accident!
B. Oh, no! Were you hurt?
A. No. But my ________(s) was/were damaged.

トンネル	**1.**	tunnel
橋	**2.**	bridge
料金所	**3.**	tollbooth
釣銭不要車両用車線	**4.**	exact change lane
案内標識	**5.**	route sign
幹線道路/高速道路	**6.**	highway
道路	**7.**	road
中央分離壁	**8.**	divider/barrier
高架路	**9.**	overpass
ガード下路	**10.**	underpass
高速道路入口	**11.**	entrance ramp/ on ramp
州間道路（高速道路）	**12.**	interstate (highway)
中央分離帯	**13.**	median
追越車線	**14.**	left lane
走行車線	**15.**	middle lane/ center lane
減速車線	**16.**	right lane
路側帯	**17.**	shoulder
車両通行帯境界線	**18.**	broken line
車両通行帯最外側線	**19.**	solid line
速度制限標識	**20.**	speed limit sign
（高速道路）出口	**21.**	exit (ramp)
出口案内標識	**22.**	exit sign
徐行標識	**23.**	yield sign
サービスエリア	**24.**	service area
踏切	**25.**	railroad crossing
街路	**26.**	street
一方通行道路	**27.**	one-way street
車道中央線	**28.**	double yellow line
横断歩道	**29.**	crosswalk
交差点	**30.**	intersection
通学用横断歩道	**31.**	school crossing
曲がり角	**32.**	corner
交通信号/信号機	**33.**	traffic light/ traffic signal
左折禁止標識	**34.**	no left turn sign
右折禁止標識	**35.**	no right turn sign
ユーターン禁止標識	**36.**	no U-turn sign
車両侵入禁止標識	**37.**	do not enter sign
一時停止標識	**38.**	stop sign

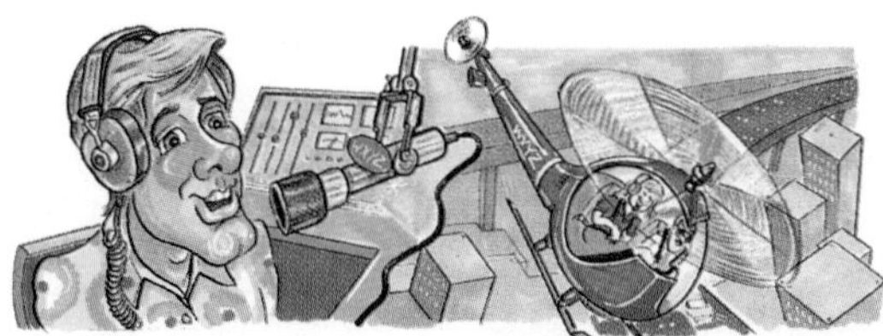

A. Where's the accident?
B. It's on/in/at/near the ______.

Describe a highway you travel on.
Describe an intersection near where you live.

In your area, on which highways and streets do most accidents occur? Why are these places dangerous?

列車 **A. train**
駅 **1.** train station
切符売り場 **2.** ticket window
(列車)発着案内板 **3.** arrival and departure board
鉄道案内所 **4.** information booth
時刻表 **5.** schedule/timetable
列車 **6.** train
線路 **7.** track
プラットホーム **8.** platform
乗客 **9.** passenger
車掌 **10.** conductor
荷物 **11.** luggage/baggage
ポーター/赤帽 **12.** porter/redcap
エンジン **13.** engine
機関士 **14.** engineer
客車 **15.** passenger car
寝台車 **16.** sleeper
食堂車 **17.** dining car

バス **B. bus**
バス **18.** bus
荷物室 **19.** luggage compartment/baggage compartment
バス運転手 **20.** bus driver
バス発着所 **21.** bus station
乗車券売場 **22.** ticket counter

市内バス **C. local bus**
バス停 **23.** bus stop
乗客 **24.** rider/passenger
運賃 **25.** (bus) fare
運賃箱 **26.** fare box
乗り換え切符 **27.** transfer

地下鉄 **D. subway**
地下鉄駅 **28.** subway station
地下鉄 **29.** subway
コイン売場 **30.** token booth
回転式改札口 **31.** turnstile
通勤客 **32.** commuter
トークン(地下鉄の切符に当たるコイン) **33.** (subway) token
フェアカード(乗車カード) **34.** fare card
フェアカード販売機 **35.** fare card machine

タクシー **E. taxi**
タクシー乗り場 **36.** taxi stand
タクシー **37.** taxi/cab/taxicab
料金メーター **38.** meter
料金 **39.** fare
タクシー運転手 **40.** cab driver/taxi driver

[A–E]
A. How are you going to get there?
B. { I'm going to take the _[A–D]_.
I'm going to take a _[E]_.

[1–8, 10–23, 26, 28–31, 35, 36]
A. Excuse me. Where's the ________?
B. Over there.

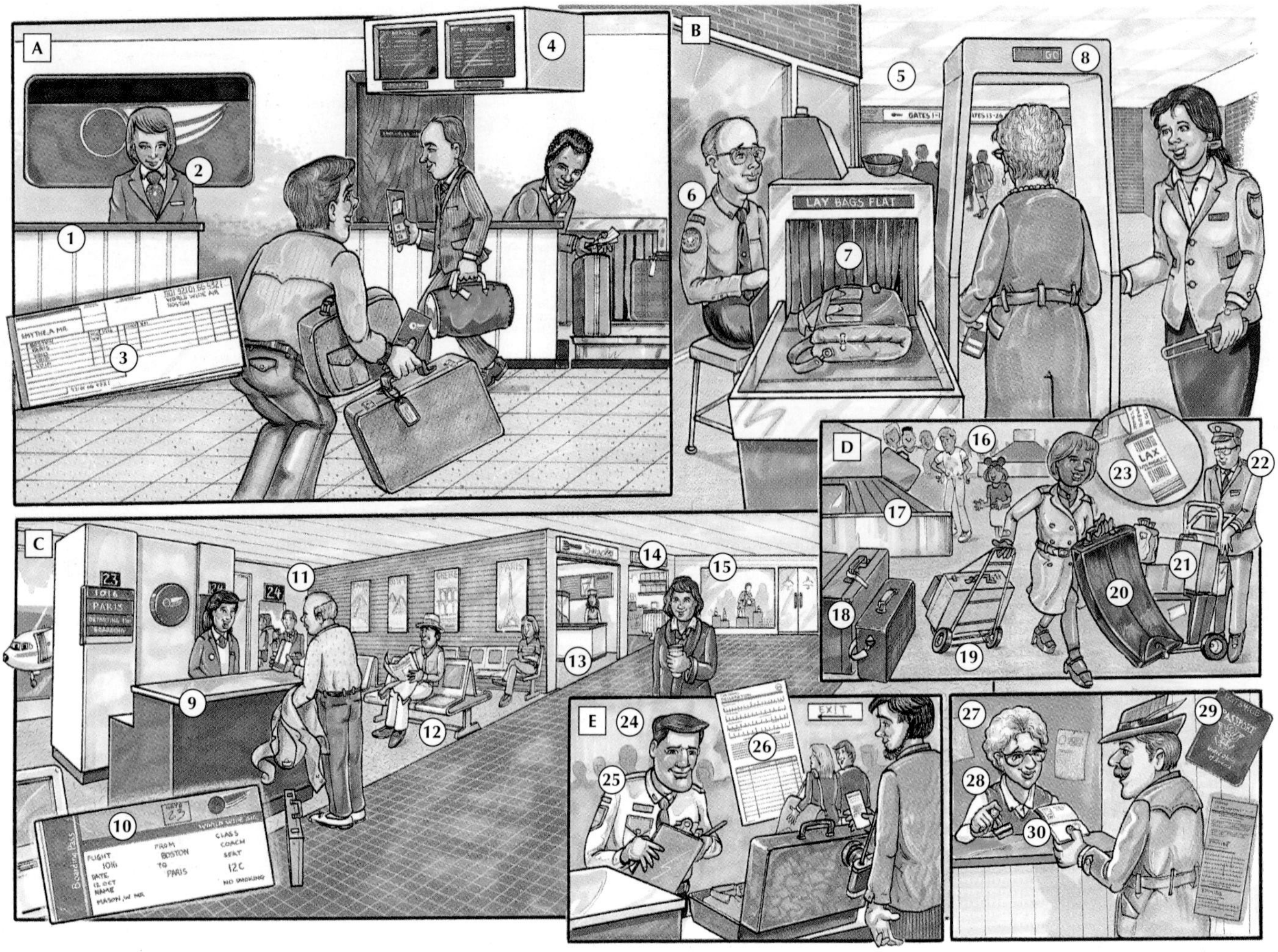

搭乗手続き **A. Check-In**
- 発券カウンター **1.** ticket counter
- 航空券取扱人 **2.** ticket agent
- 航空券 **3.** ticket
- 発着便案内表示 **4.** arrival and departure monitor

手荷物検査 **B. Security**
- 手荷物検査所 **5.** security checkpoint
- 検査官 **6.** security guard
- X線探知機 **7.** X-ray machine
- 金属探知機 **8.** metal detector

搭乗口 **C. The Gate**
- 搭乗カウンター **9.** check-in counter
- 搭乗券 **10.** boarding pass
- 搭乗口（ゲート） **11.** gate
- 待合室 **12.** waiting area
- 軽食堂 **13.** concession stand/snack bar
- 売店 **14.** gift shop
- 免税品店 **15.** duty-free shop

手荷物受取所 **D. Baggage Claim**
- 手荷物受取所 **16.** baggage claim (area)
- 回転式荷物受取台 **17.** baggage carousel
- スーツケース **18.** suitcase
- カート **19.** luggage carrier
- （スーツ携帯用）折りたたみバッグ **20.** garment bag
- 手荷物 **21.** baggage
- ポーター（手荷物取扱い係） **22.** porter/skycap
- 手荷物預り証 **23.** (baggage) claim check

税関と入国審査 **E. Customs and Immigration**
- 税関 **24.** customs
- 税官吏 **25.** customs officer
- 税関申告書 **26.** customs declaration form
- 入国審査所 **27.** immigration
- 入国審査官 **28.** immigration officer
- パスポート **29.** passport
- ビザ（査証） **30.** visa

[1, 2, 4–9, 11–17, 24, 25, 27, 28]

A. Excuse me. Where's the _______?*

B. Right over there.

[3, 10, 18–21, 23, 26, 29, 30]

A. Oh, no! I think I've lost my _______!

B. I'll help you look for it.

*With 24 and 27, use: Excuse me. Where's _______?

操縦室 **1.** cockpit
機長 **2.** pilot/captain
副操縦士 **3.** co-pilot
計器パネル **4.** instrument panel
航空機関士 **5.** flight engineer
ファーストクラス客室 **6.** first-class section
乗客 **7.** passenger
調理室 **8.** galley
乗務員 **9.** flight attendant
トイレ **10.** lavatory/bathroom
客室 **11.** cabin
機内持ち込み手荷物 **12.** carry-on bag
荷物棚 **13.** overhead compartment
通路 **14.** aisle
シートベルト **15.** seat belt
窓側座席 **16.** window seat
中央座席 **17.** middle seat
通路側座席 **18.** aisle seat
シートベルト着用ランプ **19.** Fasten Seat Belt sign
禁煙ランプ **20.** No Smoking sign
呼出しボタン **21.** call button
酸素マスク **22.** oxygen mask
非常口 **23.** emergency exit
ひじ掛け **24.** armrest
リクライニングレバー **25.** seat control
テーブル **26.** tray (table)
食事 **27.** meal
小物入れ **28.** seat pocket
非常時手引き書 **29.** emergency instruction card
汚物処理袋 **30.** air sickness bag
救命胴衣 **31.** life vest
滑走路 **32.** runway
空港ターミナル **33.** terminal (building)
管制塔 **34.** control tower
飛行機（ジェット機） **35.** airplane/plane/jet
機首 **36.** nose
機体 **37.** fuselage
貨物搬入口 **38.** cargo door
車輪 **39.** landing gear
主翼 **40.** wing
エンジン **41.** engine
尾部 **42.** tail
プロペラ機 **43.** propeller plane/prop
プロペラ **44.** propeller
ヘリコプター **45.** helicopter
回転翼 **46.** rotor (blade)

A. Where's the _______?
B. In/On/Next to/Behind/In front of/Above/Below the _______.

Ladies and gentlemen. This is your captain speaking. I'm sorry for the delay. We had a little problem with one of our _______s.* Everything is fine now and we'll be taking off shortly.

**Use 4, 7, 10, 12, 20–22, 24.*

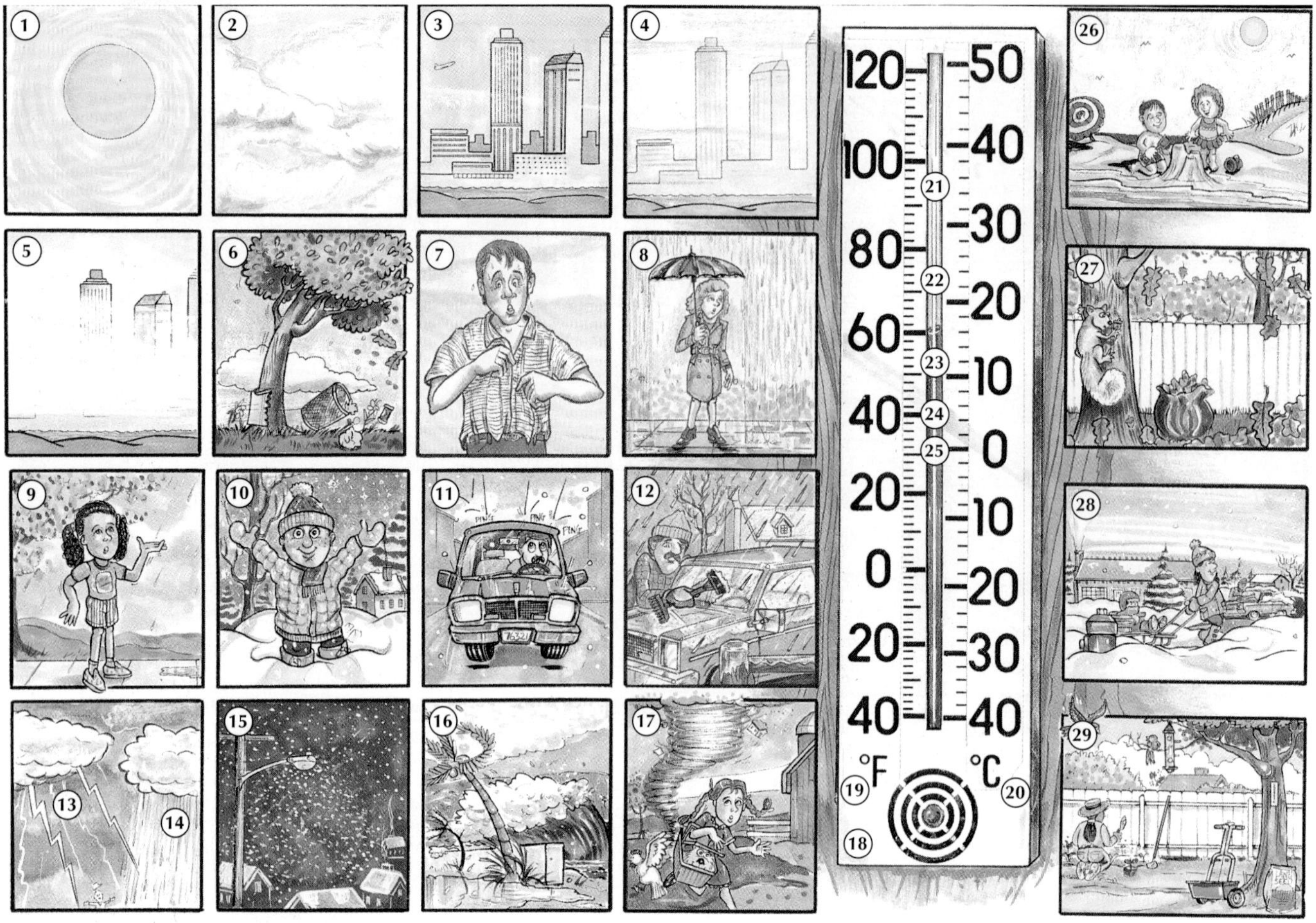

天候 A. Weather

- 快晴の **1.** sunny
- 曇った **2.** cloudy
- 晴れた **3.** clear
- もやのかかった **4.** hazy
- 霧の深い **5.** foggy
- 風の強い **6.** windy
- じめじめした/むし暑い **7.** humid/muggy
- 雨降りの **8.** raining
- 霧雨の降る **9.** drizzling
- 雪の降る **10.** snowing
- あられの降る **11.** hailing
- ひょうの降る **12.** sleeting
- 稲妻が光る **13.** lightning
- 雷雨 **14.** thunderstorm
- 吹雪 **15.** snowstorm
- ハリケーン/台風 **16.** hurricane/typhoon
- たつ巻 **17.** tornado

気温 B. Temperature

- 温度計 **18.** thermometer
- 華氏 **19.** Fahrenheit
- 摂氏 **20.** Centigrade/Celsius
- 暑い **21.** hot
- 暖かい **22.** warm
- 涼しい **23.** cool
- 寒い **24.** cold
- 凍えそうな **25.** freezing

季節 C. Seasons

- 夏 **26.** summer
- 秋 **27.** fall/autumn
- 冬 **28.** winter
- 春 **29.** spring

[1–12]
A. What's the weather like?
B. It's ________.

[13–17]
A. What's the weather forecast?
B. There's going to be
[13] /a [14–17] .

[19–25]
A. How's the weather?
B. It's [21–25] .
A. What's the temperature?
B. It's .... degrees [19, 20] .

Describe the seasons where you live.
Tell about the weather and the temperature.

What's your favorite season?
Why?

キャンプ **A. camping**
- テント **1.** tent
- リュックサック/バックパック **2.** backpack
- 寝袋 **3.** sleeping bag
- くい **4.** tent stakes
- おの **5.** hatchet
- ランプ **6.** lantern
- キャンプ用携帯こんろ **7.** camp stove

ハイキング **B. hiking**
- 登山靴 **8.** hiking boots
- コンパス/羅針盤 **9.** compass
- 地図 **10.** trail map

登山 **C. mountain climbing**
- 登山靴 **11.** hiking boots

ロッククライミング/岩登り **D. rock climbing**
- ロープ **12.** rope
- 背負い革 **13.** harness

ピクニック **E. picnic**
- ピクニックシート **14.** (picnic) blanket
- 魔法びん **15.** thermos
- ピクニックバスケット **16.** picnic basket

[A–E]
A. Let's go _______* this weekend.
B. Good idea! We haven't gone _______* in a long time.

With E, say: on a picnic

[1–16]
A. Did you bring the _______?
B. Yes, I did.

Have you ever gone camping or hiking? Where? What equipment did you use?

Do you like to go on picnics? Where? What picnic supplies and food do you take with you?

ジョギングコース **1.** jogging path
トイレ **2.** rest rooms
彫像 **3.** statue
ピクニック場 **4.** picnic area
ピクニック用テーブル **5.** picnic table
グリル **6.** grill
ごみ入れ **7.** trash can
メリーゴーランド/回転木馬 **8.** merry-go-round/carousel
噴水 **9.** fountain

動物園 **10.** zoo
水飲み場 **11.** water fountain
野外音楽堂 **12.** band shell
乗馬道 **13.** bridle path
駐輪場 **14.** bike rack
池 **15.** duck pond
サイクリングコース **16.** bicycle path/bikeway
ベンチ **17.** bench
遊び場 **18.** playground

ジャングルジム **19.** jungle gym
うんてい **20.** monkey bars
すべり台 **21.** slide
ブランコ **22.** swings
タイヤブランコ **23.** tire swing
シーソー **24.** seesaw
水遊び場 **25.** wading pool
砂場 **26.** sandbox
砂 **27.** sand

[1–18]

A. Excuse me. Does this park have (a) ________?

B. Yes. Right over there.

A. { Be careful on the [19–24] !
Be careful in the [25–27] !

B. I will, Mom/Dad.

Describe a park and a playground you are familiar with.

救助員 **1.** lifeguard
看視台 **2.** lifeguard stand
救命具 **3.** life preserver
売店 **4.** snack bar/refresh-ment stand
砂丘 **5.** sand dune
岩場 **6.** rock
遊泳者 **7.** swimmer
波 **8.** wave
サーファー **9.** surfer
物売り **10.** vendor

日光浴をしている人 **11.** sunbather
砂の城 **12.** sand castle
貝殻 **13.** seashell/shell
ビーチパラソル **14.** beach umbrella
デッキチェア **15.** (beach) chair
ビーチタオル **16.** (beach) towel
水着 **17.** bathing suit/ swimsuit
水泳帽 **18.** bathing cap
ビート板 **19.** kickboard
サーフボード **20.** surfboard
たこ **21.** kite

空気マット **22.** raft/air mattress
浮き輪 **23.** tube
レジャーシート **24.** (beach) blanket
日よけ帽子 **25.** sun hat
サングラス **26.** sunglasses
日焼け止めローション **27.** suntan lotion/ sunscreen
バケツ **28.** pail/bucket
シャベル **29.** shovel
ビーチボール **30.** beach ball
アイスボックス **31.** cooler

[1–13]
A. What a nice beach!
B. It is. Look at all the _______s!

[14–31]
A. Are you ready for the beach?
B. Almost. I just have to get my _______.

Do you like to go to the beach? Describe your favorite beach. What do you take when you go there?

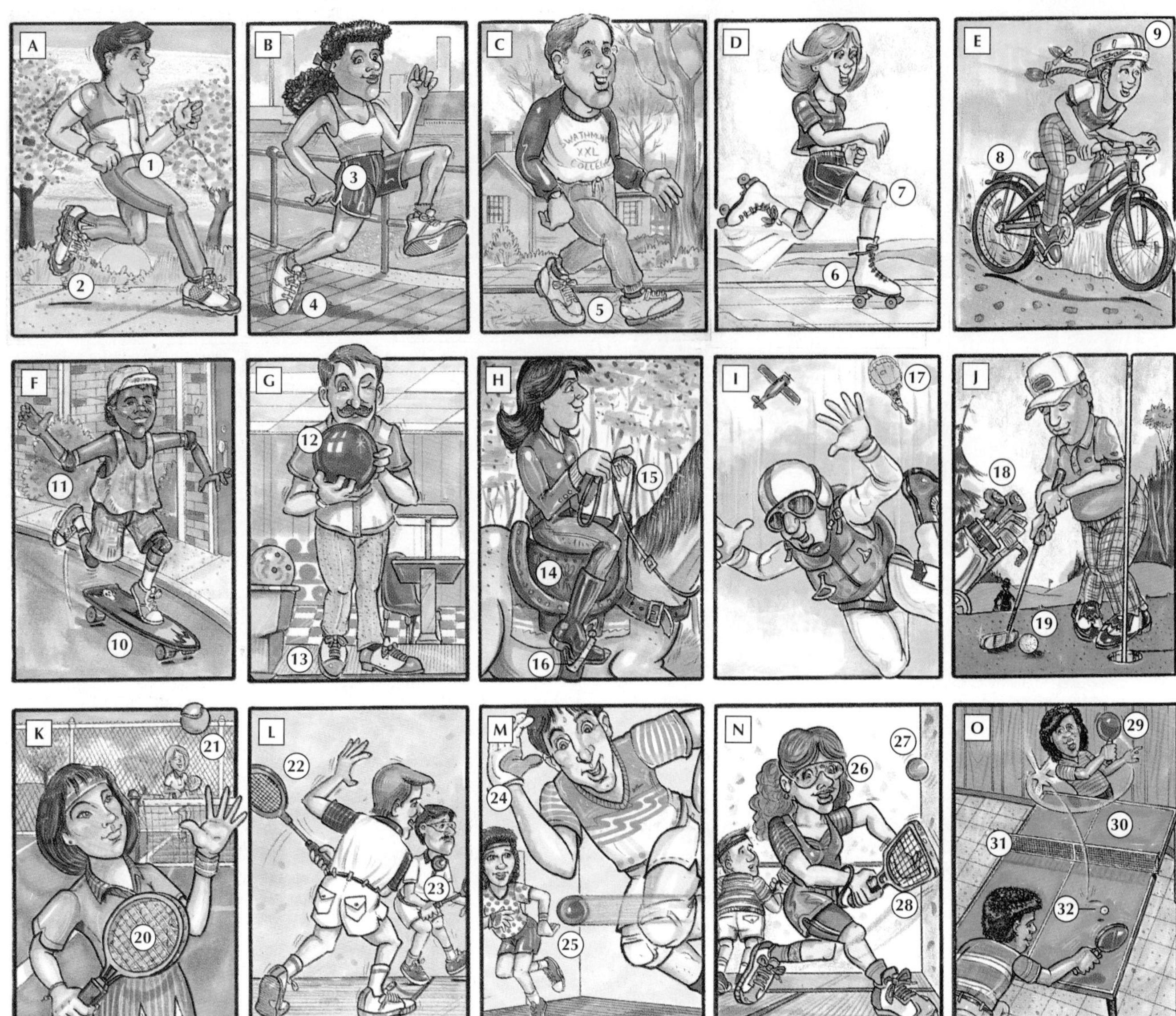

ジョギング **A. jogging**
ジョギングスーツ **1.** jogging suit
ジョギングシューズ **2.** jogging shoes

ランニング **B. running**
ランニングパンツ **3.** running shorts
ランニングシューズ **4.** running shoes

ウォーキング **C. walking**
ウォーキングシューズ **5.** walking shoes

ローラースケート **D. roller skating**
ローラースケート **6.** roller skates
ひざ当て **7.** knee pads

サイクリング **E. cycling/bicycling/biking**
自転車 **8.** bicycle/bike
ヘルメット **9.** (bicycle) helmet

スケートボード **F. skateboarding**
スケートボード **10.** skateboard
ひじ当て **11.** elbow pads

ボウリング **G. bowling**
ボウリングボール **12.** bowling ball
ボウリングシューズ **13.** bowling shoes

乗馬 **H. horseback riding**
くら **14.** saddle
手綱 **15.** reins
あぶみ **16.** stirrups

スカイダイビング **I. skydiving**
パラシュート **17.** parachute

ゴルフ **J. golf**
クラブ **18.** golf clubs
ゴルフボール **19.** golf ball

テニス **K. tennis**
テニスラケット **20.** tennis racquet
テニスボール **21.** tennis ball

スカッシュ **L. squash**
スカッシュラケット **22.** squash racquet
スカッシュボール **23.** squash ball

アメリカ式ハンドボール **M. handball**
グローブ **24.** handball glove
ハンドボール **25.** handball

ラケットボール **N. racquetball**
保護ゴーグル **26.** safety goggles
ラケットボール **27.** racquetball
ラケット **28.** racquet

卓球 **O. ping pong**
ラケット **29.** paddle
卓球台 **30.** ping pong table
ネット **31.** net
卓球ボール/ピンポン玉 **32.** ping pong ball

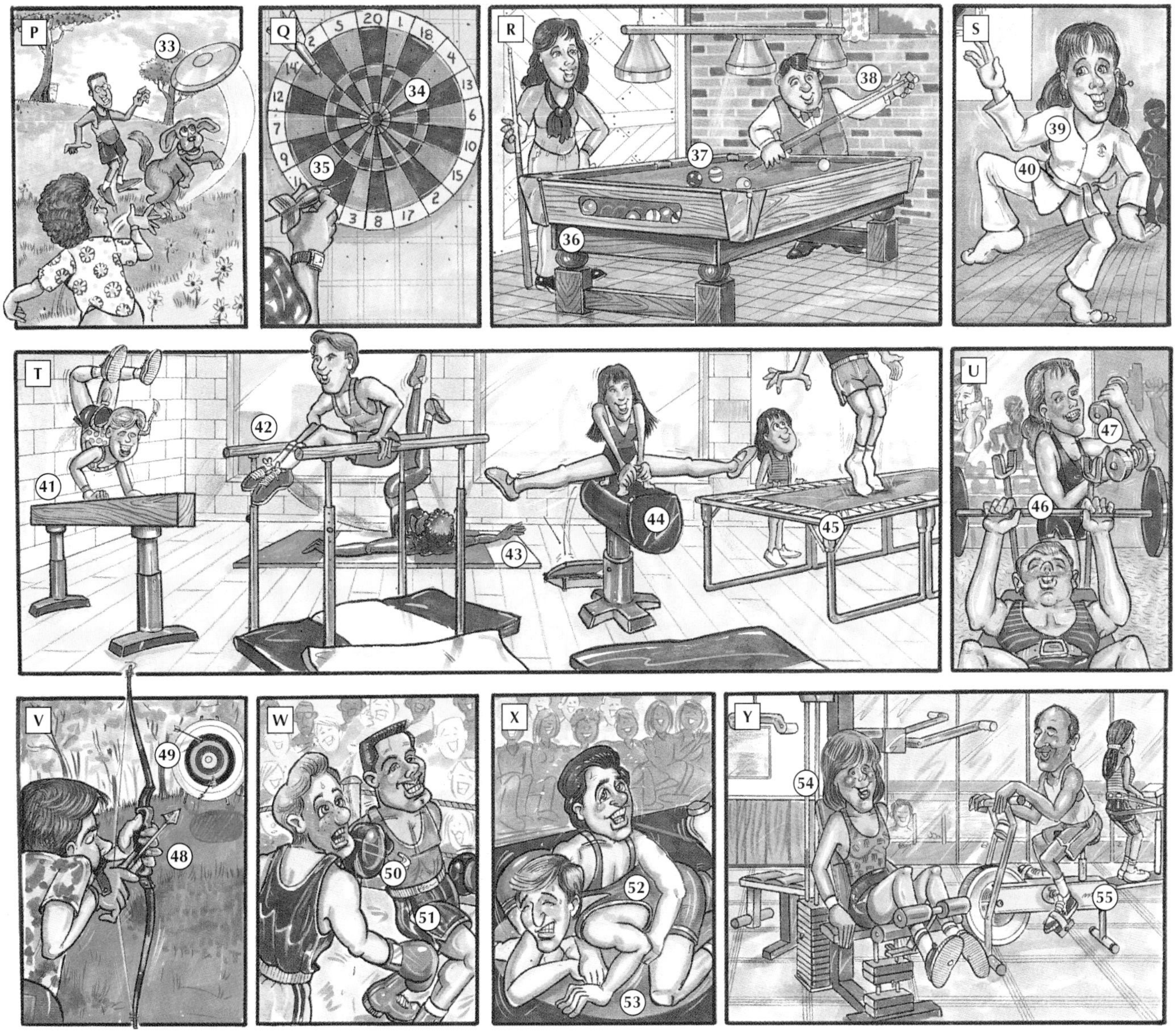

フリスビー **P. frisbee**
フリスビー **33.** frisbee

ダーツ **Q. darts**
ダーツボード/ダーツ盤 **34.** dartboard
ダーツ **35.** darts

ビリヤード **R. billiards/pool**
ビリヤード台 **36.** pool table
ビリヤードの球 **37.** billiard balls
キュー **38.** pool stick

空手 **S. karate**
空手道衣 **39.** karate outfit
帯 **40.** karate belt

体操 **T. gymnastics**
平均台 **41.** balance beam
平行棒 **42.** parallel bars
ゆか **43.** mat
鞍馬（跳馬） **44.** horse
トランポリン **45.** trampoline

ウェイトリフティング **U. weightlifting**
バーベル **46.** barbell
ウェイト（鉄アレー） **47.** weights

アーチェリー **V. archery**
弓矢 **48.** bow and arrow
標的 **49.** target

ボクシング **W. box**
ボクシンググローブ **50.** boxing gloves
トランクス **51.** (boxing) trunks

レスリング **X. wrestle**
レスリングユニフォーム **52.** wrestling uniform
マット **53.** (wrestling) mat

トレーニング/フィットネス **Y. work out**
多機能エクササイズマシーン **54.** universal/ exercise equipment
エアロバイク **55.** exercise bike

[A–Y]
A. What do you like to do in your free time?
B. I like to go [A–I].
I like to play [J–R].
I like to do [S–V].
I like to [W–Y].

[1–55]
A. I really like this/these new ________.
B. It's/They're very nice.

[A–F]
A. Do you like **baseball**?
B. Yes. **Baseball** is one of my favorite sports.

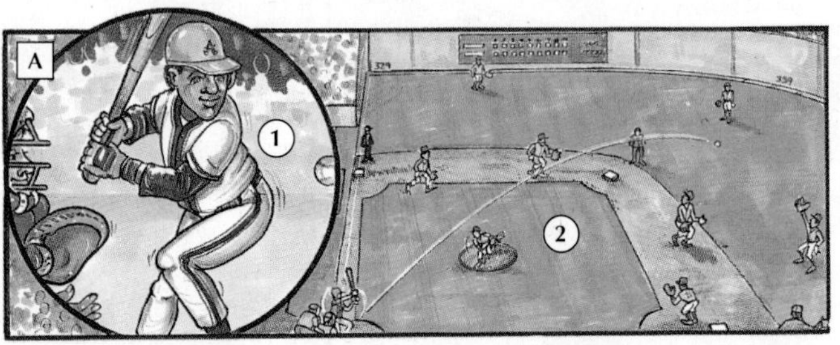

野球 **A. baseball**
野球選手 **1.** baseball player
球場 **2.** baseball field/ballfield

ソフトボール **B. softball**
ソフトボール選手 **3.** softball player
球場 **4.** ballfield

アメリカンフットボール **C. football**
アメリカンフットボール選手 **5.** football player
アメリカンフットボール競技場 **6.** football field

ラクロス **D. lacrosse**
ラクロス選手 **7.** lacrosse player
ラクロス競技場 **8.** lacrosse field

アイスホッケー **E. (ice) hockey**
アイスホッケー選手 **9.** hockey player
アイスホッケーリンク **10.** hockey rink

バスケットボール **F. basketball**
バスケット選手 **11.** basketball player
バスケットコート **12.** basketball court

バレーボール **G. volleyball**
バレー選手 **13.** volleyball player
バレーコート **14.** volleyball court

サッカー **H. soccer**
サッカー選手 **15.** soccer player
サッカー場 **16.** soccer field

A. .... plays [A–H] very well.
B. You're right. I think he's/she's one of the best ________s* on the team.

**Use 1, 3, 5, 7, 9, 11, 13, 15.*

A. Now, listen! I want all of you to go out on that ________† and play the best game of [A–H] you've ever played!
B. All right, Coach!

†Use 2, 4, 6, 8, 10, 12, 14, 16.

Which sports on this page do you like to play? Which do you like to watch?
What are your favorite teams?
Name some famous players of these sports.

[1–26]
A. I can't find my **baseball**!
B. Look in the *closet*.*

*closet, basement, garage

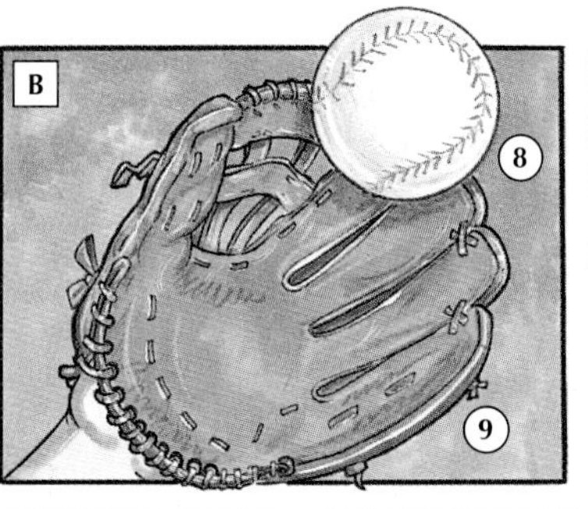

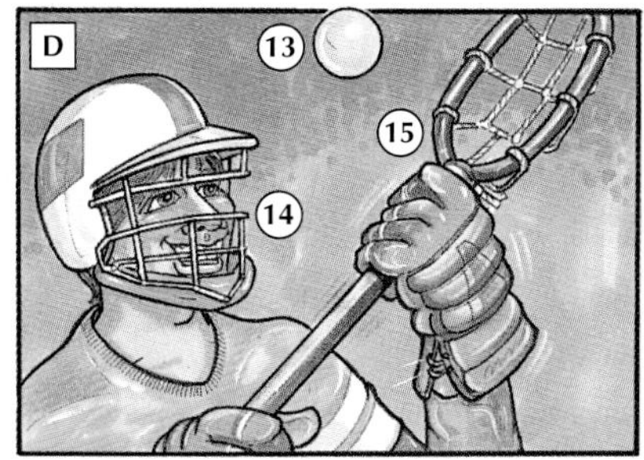

野球 **A. baseball**
野球ボール **1.** baseball
バット **2.** bat
ヘルメット **3.** batting helmet
野球ユニフォーム **4.** baseball uniform
キャッチャーマスク **5.** catcher's mask
グローブ **6.** baseball glove
キャッチャーミット **7.** catcher's mit

ソフトボール **B. softball**
ソフトボール **8.** softball
グラブ **9.** softball glove

アメリカンフットボール **C. football**
フットボール **10.** football
ヘルメット **11.** football helmet
肩パッド **12.** shoulder pads

ラクロス **D. lacrosse**
ラクロスボール **13.** lacrosse ball
ヘルメット **14.** face guard
スティック **15.** lacrosse stick

アイスホッケー **E. hockey**
ホッケーパック **16.** hockey puck
ホッケースティック **17.** hockey stick
フェイスマスク **18.** hockey mask
ホッケーグローブ **19.** hockey glove
ホッケー用スケート靴 **20.** hockey skates

バスケットボール **F. basketball**
バスケットボール **21.** basketball
バックボード **22.** backboard
ゴール **23.** basketball hoop

バレーボール **G. volleyball**
バレーボール **24.** volleyball
ネット **25.** volleyball net

サッカー **H. soccer**
サッカーボール **26.** soccer ball
すね当て **27.** shinguards

[In a store]
A. Excuse me. I'm looking for (a) [1–27].
B. All our [A–H] equipment is over there.
A. Thanks.

[At home]
A. I'm going to play [A–H] after school today.
B. Don't forget your [1–21, 24–27]!

Which sports on this page are popular in your country? Which sports are played in high school?

[A–H]
A. What's your favorite winter sport?
B. **Skiing**.

スキー **A. (downhill) skiing**
スキー板 **1.** skis
スキー靴 **2.** ski boots
ビンディング **3.** bindings
ストック **4.** poles

クロスカントリースキー **B. cross-country skiing**
クロスカントリー用スキー板 **5.** cross-country skis

スケート **C. (ice) skating**
スケート靴 **6.** (ice) skates
エッジカバー **7.** skate guards

フィギュアスケート **D. figure skating**
フィギュア用スケート靴 **8.** figure skates

そりすべり **E. sledding**
そり **9.** sled
丸ぞり **10.** sledding dish/saucer

ボブスレー **F. bobsledding**
ボブスレー **11.** bobsled

スノーモービル **G. snowmobiling**
スノーモービル **12.** snowmobile

リュージュ/トボガン **H. tobogganing**
リュージュ/トボガン **13.** toboggan

[A–H]
[At work or at school on Friday]
A. What are you going to do this weekend?
B. I'm going to go ________.

[1–13]
[On the telephone]
A. Hello. Jimmy's Sporting Goods.
B. Hello. Do you sell ________(s)?
A. Yes, we do./No, we don't.

Have you ever watched the Winter Olympics? What is your favorite event? Which event do you think is the most exciting? the most dangerous?

[A–L]
A. Would you like to go **sailing** tomorrow?
B. Sure. I'd love to.

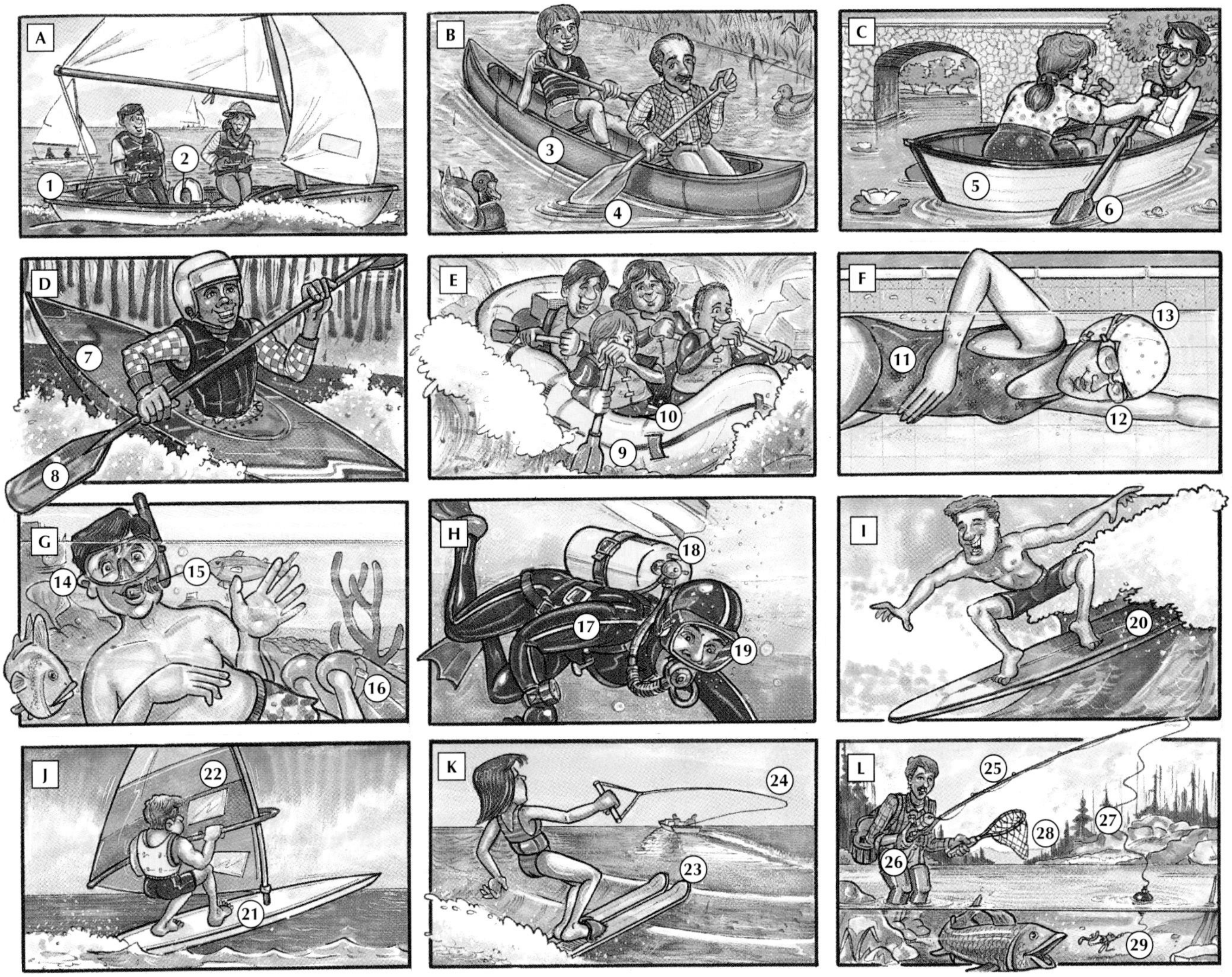

ヨット **A. sailing**
ヨット **1.** sailboat
救命具 **2.** life preserver

カヌー **B. canoeing**
カヌー **3.** canoe
パドル **4.** paddles

ボート **C. rowing**
手こぎボート **5.** rowboat
オール **6.** oars

カヤック **D. kayaking**
カヤック **7.** kayak
パドル **8.** paddle

ラフティング(川下り) **E. (white water) rafting**
ゴムボート(いかだ) **9.** raft
救命胴衣 **10.** life jacket

水泳 **F. swimming**
水着 **11.** swimsuit/bathing suit
ゴーグル **12.** goggles
水泳帽 **13.** bathing cap

シュノーケリング **G. snorkeling**
水中めがね **14.** mask
シュノーケル **15.** snorkel
足ひれ **16.** flippers

スキューバダイビング **H. scuba diving**
ウエットスーツ **17.** wet suit
酸素ボンベ **18.** (air) tank
潜水マスク **19.** (diving) mask

サーフィン **I. surfing**
サーフボード **20.** surfboard

ウインドサーフィン **J. windsurfing**
セイルボード **21.** sailboard
帆 **22.** sail

水上スキー **K. waterskiing**
水上用スキー板 **23.** water skis
引き綱 **24.** towrope

釣り **L. fishing**
釣りざお **25.** (fishing) rod
リール **26.** reel
釣り糸 **27.** (fishing) line
網 **28.** net
えさ **29.** bait

A. Have you ever gone [A–L]?
B. Yes, I have./No, I haven't.

A. Do you have everything you need to go [A–L]?
B. Yes. I have my [1–29] (and my [1–29]).
A. Have a good time.

Which sports on this page have you tried? Which sports would you like to try? Are any of these sports popular in your country? Which ones?

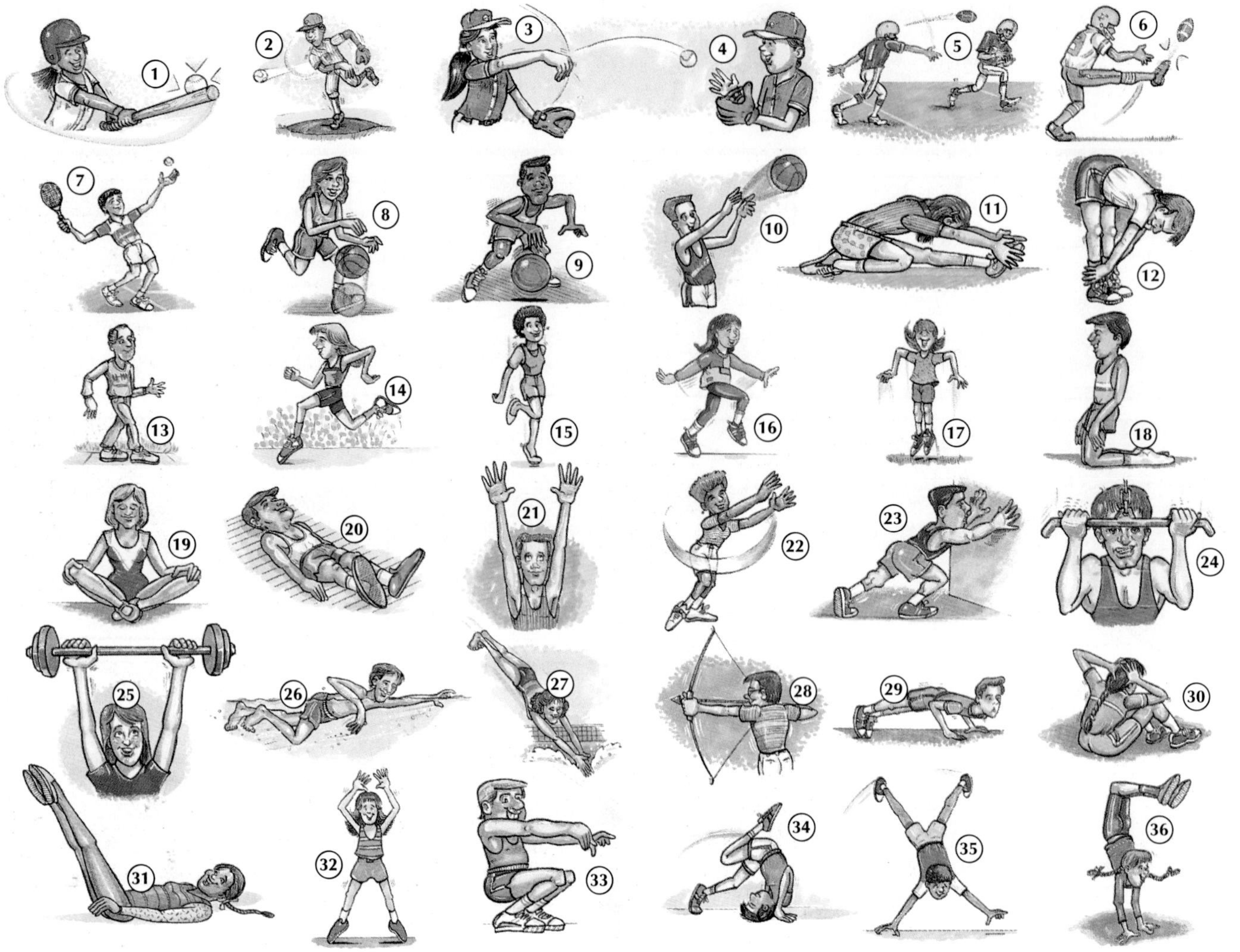

打つ **1.** hit
投球する **2.** pitch
投げる **3.** throw
つかむ **4.** catch
パスする **5.** pass
蹴る **6.** kick
サーブする **7.** serve
バウンドする **8.** bounce
ドリブルする **9.** dribble
シュートする **10.** shoot
伸ばす **11.** stretch
曲げる **12.** bend

歩く **13.** walk
走る **14.** run
ぴょんととぶ/（片足で）とぶ **15.** hop
スキップする **16.** skip
ジャンプする（とび上がる） **17.** jump
ひざをつく **18.** kneel
すわる **19.** sit
横になる **20.** lie down
腕を伸ばす **21.** reach
腕をふる **22.** swing
押す **23.** push
引く **24.** pull

もち上げる **25.** lift
泳ぐ **26.** swim
飛びこむ **27.** dive
射る **28.** shoot
腕立て伏せ **29.** push-up
上体起こし/腹筋運動 **30.** sit-up
脚上げ **31.** leg lift
ジャンピングジャック（準備体操の一種） **32.** jumping jack
ひざの屈伸 **33.** deep knee bend
宙返り/とんぼ返り/回転 **34.** somersault
側転 **35.** cartwheel
逆立ち **36.** handstand

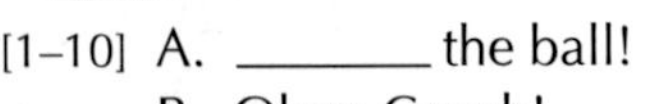

[1–10] A. ________ the ball!
B. Okay, Coach!

[11–28] A. Now ________!
B. Like this?
A. Yes.

[29–36] A. Okay, everybody. I want you to do twenty ________s!
B. Twenty ________s?!
A. That's right.

Do you exercise regularly?
Which exercises do you do?

Be an exercise instructor. Lead your friends in an exercise routine using the actions on this page.

[A–Q]
A. What's your hobby?
B. **Sewing.**

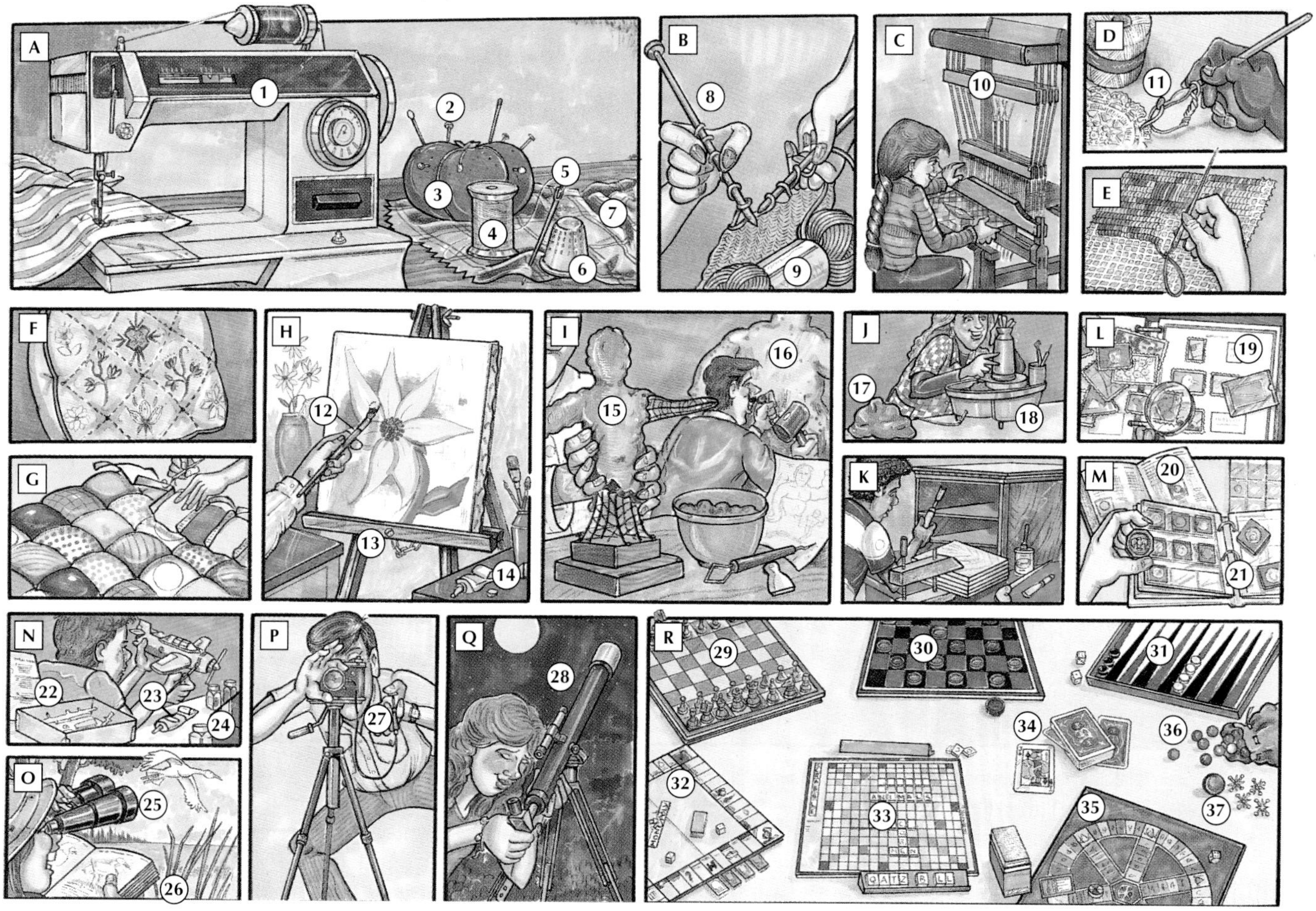

裁縫 **A. sewing**
ミシン 1. sewing machine
待ち針 2. pin
針さし 3. pin cushion
糸 4. thread
縫い針 5. (sewing) needle
指ぬき 6. thimble
布地 7. material
編み物 **B. knitting**
編み棒 8. knitting needle
編み糸 9. yarn
織物 **C. weaving**
織物機 10. loom
かぎ針編み **D. crocheting**
かぎ針 11. crochet hook
ニードルポイントレース **E. needlepoint**
刺しゅう **F. embroidery**
キルティング **G. quilting**

絵画 **H. painting**
絵筆 12. paintbrush
イーゼル 13. easel
絵の具 14. paint
彫刻 **I. sculpting/sculpture**
石こう 15. plaster
石材 16. stone
陶芸 **J. pottery**
粘土 17. clay
ろくろ 18. potter's wheel
木工 **K. woodworking**
切手収集 **L. stamp collecting**
切手アルバム 19. stamp album
コイン収集 **M. coin collecting**
コインカタログ 20. coin catalog
コインアルバム 21. coin album
プラモデル **N. model building**
プラモデル 22. model kit

接着剤 23. (model) glue
ペンキ 24. (model) paint
バードウォッチング(野鳥観察) **O. bird watching**
双眼鏡 25. binoculars
フィールドガイド 26. field guide
写真 **P. photography**
カメラ 27. camera
天文 **Q. astronomy**
天体望遠鏡 28. telescope
ゲーム **R. games**
チェス 29. chess
チェッカー 30. checkers
バックギャモン 31. backgammon
モノポリー 32. Monopoly
スクラブル 33. Scrabble
トランプ 34. cards
トリビアル・パースー 35. Trivial Pursuit
おはじき 36. marbles
ジャックス 37. jacks

[1–28] [In a store]
A. May I help you?
B. Yes, please. I'd like to buy (a/an) ________.

[29–37] [At home]
A. What do you want to do?
B. Let's play ________.

What's your hobby?
What games are popular in your country? Describe how to play one.

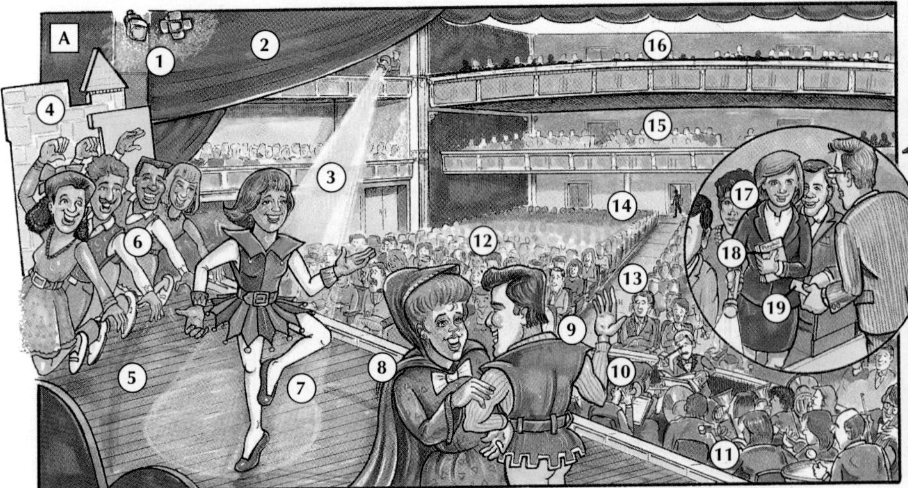

劇場 **A. theater**
照明 **1.** lights/lighting
幕 **2.** curtain
スポットライト **3.** spotlight
背景 **4.** scenery
舞台 **5.** stage
コーラス **6.** chorus
ダンサー **7.** dancer
女優 **8.** actress
男優 **9.** actor
管弦楽団(オーケストラ) **10.** orchestra
オーケストラボックス **11.** orchestra pit
観衆 **12.** audience
通路 **13.** aisle
一階正面席 **14.** orchestra
二階正面席 **15.** mezzanine
桟敷 **16.** balcony
案内係 **17.** usher
プログラム **18.** program
入場券 **19.** ticket

交響曲演奏会 **B. symphony**
交響楽団 **20.** symphony orchestra
演奏者 **21.** musician
指揮者 **22.** conductor
指揮棒 **23.** baton
指揮台 **24.** podium

オペラ **C. opera**
オペラ歌手 **25.** opera singer
オペラ団 **26.** opera company

バレエ **D. ballet**
バレエダンサー **27.** ballet dancer
バレリーナ **28.** ballerina
バレエ団 **29.** ballet company
バレエシューズ **30.** ballet slippers
トウシューズ **31.** toeshoes

映画 **E. movies**
(劇場等の出入口の)ひさし **32.** marquee
入場券売場 **33.** box office
広告板 **34.** billboard
ロビー **35.** lobby
売店 **36.** refreshment stand
スクリーン **37.** (movie) screen

[A–E]
A. What are you doing this evening?
B. I'm going to the .

[1–11, 20–37]
A. { What a magnificent ________!
 What magnificent 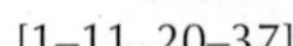s!
B. I agree.

[14–16]
A. Where did you sit during the performance?
B. We sat in the ________.

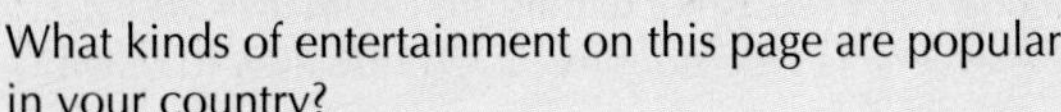

What kinds of entertainment on this page are popular in your country?

Tell about a play, concert, opera, ballet, or movie you have seen. Describe the performance and the theater.

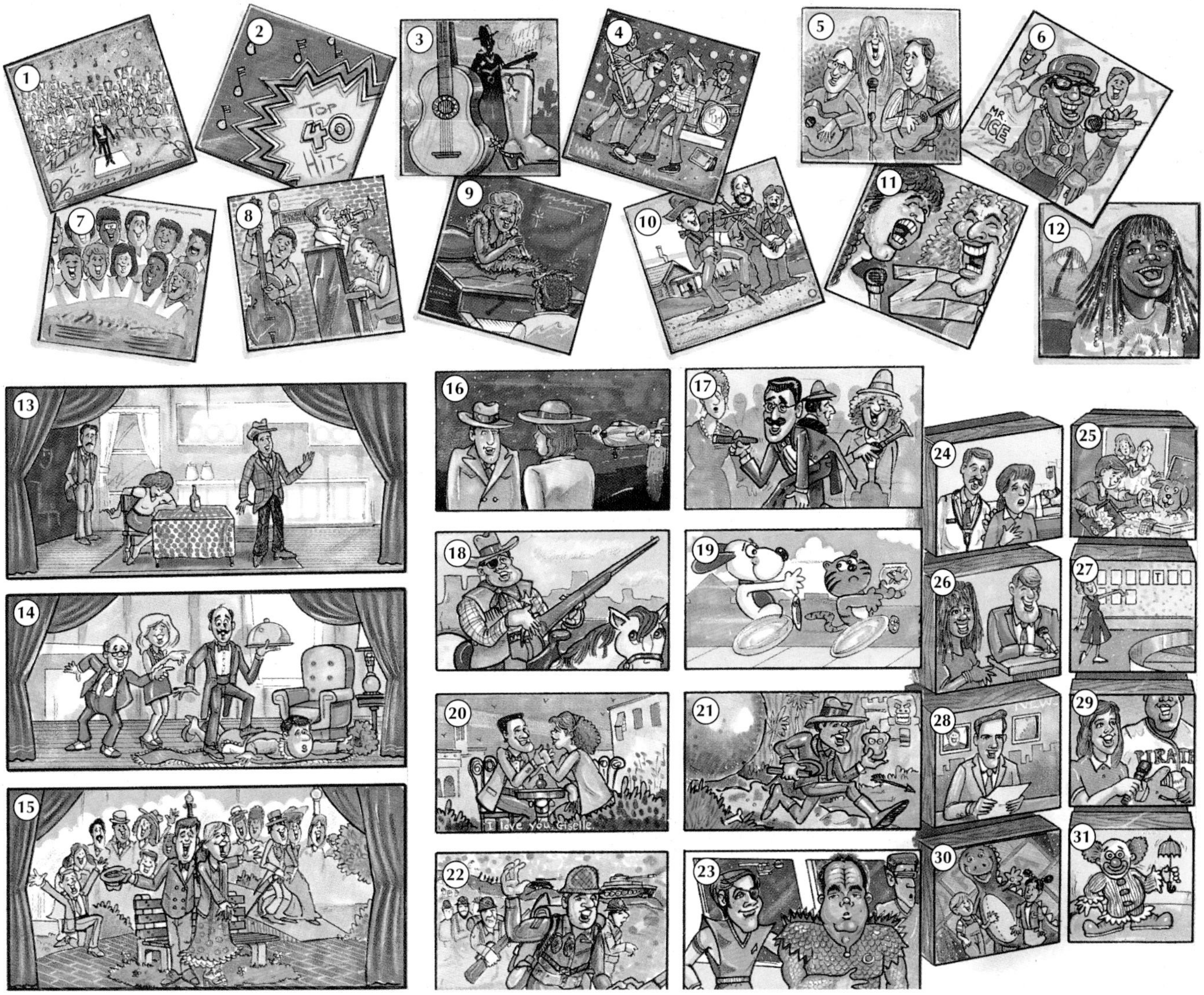

音楽 **A. music**
- クラシック **1.** classical music
- ポピュラー **2.** popular music
- カントリー **3.** country music
- ロック **4.** rock music
- フォーク **5.** folk music
- ラップ **6.** rap music
- ゴスペル **7.** gospel music
- ジャズ **8.** jazz
- ブルース **9.** blues
- ブルーグラス **10.** bluegrass
- ヘビーメタル **11.** heavy metal
- レゲエ **12.** reggae

演劇 **B. plays**
- ドラマ **13.** drama
- 喜劇 **14.** comedy
- ミュージカル **15.** musical (comedy)

映画 **C. movies**
- ドラマ **16.** drama
- 喜劇 **17.** comedy
- 西部劇 **18.** western
- アニメーション **19.** cartoon
- 外国映画 **20.** foreign film
- 冒険映画 **21.** adventure movie
- 戦争映画 **22.** war movie
- SF映画 **23.** science fiction movie

テレビ番組 **D. TV programs**
- ドラマ **24.** drama
- コメディー番組 **25.** (situation) comedy/sitcom
- 対談番組 **26.** talk show
- クイズ・ゲーム番組 **27.** game show
- ニュース番組 **28.** news program
- スポーツ番組 **29.** sports program
- 子供向番組 **30.** children's program
- アニメ番組 **31.** cartoon

A. What kind of [A–D] do you like?
B. { I like [1–12].
{ I like [13–31]s.

What's your favorite type of music?
Who is your favorite singer? musician? musical group?

What kind of movies do you like?
Who are your favorite movie stars?
What are the titles of your favorite movies?

What kind of TV programs do you like?
What are your favorite shows?

A. Do you play a musical instrument?
B. Yes. I play the **violin**.

A. Strings 弦楽器
1. violin バイオリン
2. viola ビオラ
3. cello チェロ
4. bass コントラバス
5. (acoustic) guitar ギター
6. ukelele ウクレレ
7. electric guitar エレキギター
8. banjo バンジョー
9. mandolin マンドリン
10. harp ハープ

B. Woodwinds 木管楽器
11. piccolo ピッコロ
12. flute フルート
13. clarinet クラリネット
14. oboe オーボエ
15. recorder リコーダー
16. saxophone サクソホン
17. bassoon バスーン

C. Brass 金管楽器
18. trumpet トランペット
19. trombone トロンボーン
20. French horn フレンチホルン
21. tuba チューバ

D. Percussion 打楽器
22. drum 太鼓
23. kettle drum ケトルドラム/ティンパニ
24. bongos ボンゴ
25. conga (drum) コンガ
26. cymbals シンバル
27. xylophone シロホン/木琴

E. Keyboard Instruments 鍵盤楽器
28. piano ピアノ
29. organ オルガン
30. electric piano/ digital piano 電子ピアノ
31. synthesizer シンセサイザー

F. Other Instruments その他の楽器
32. accordion アコーディオン
33. harmonica ハーモニカ

A. You play the ______ very well.
B. Thank you.

A. What's that noise?
B. That's my son/daughter practicing the ______.

Do you play a musical instrument? Which one?
Name and describe other musical instruments used in your country.

木 **1.** tree
葉 **2.** leaf-leaves
小枝 **3.** twig
枝 **4.** branch
大枝 **5.** limb
幹 **6.** trunk
樹皮 **7.** bark
根 **8.** root
針状葉 **9.** needle
球果（松ぼっくりなど） **10.** cone
ハナミズキ **11.** dogwood
ヒイラギ **12.** holly
モクレン **13.** magnolia
ニレ **14.** elm
サクラ **15.** cherry
ヤシ **16.** palm
カバ **17.** birch

カエデ **18.** maple
ナラ・カシなど **19.** oak
マツ **20.** pine
アカスギ **21.** redwood
ヤナギ **22.** (weeping) willow
花 **23.** flower
花びら **24.** petal
めしべ **25.** pistula
おしべ **26.** stamen
茎 **27.** stem
つぼみ **28.** bud
とげ **29.** thorn
球根 **30.** bulb
キク **31.** chrysanthemum/ mum
ラッパスイセン **32.** daffodil
ヒナギク **33.** daisy

クチナシ **34.** gardenia
ユリ **35.** lily
パンジー **36.** pansy
ペチュニア **37.** petunia
ラン **38.** orchid
バラ **39.** rose
ヒマワリ **40.** sunflower
チューリップ **41.** tulip
スミレ **42.** violet
低木/低木のしげみ **43.** bush
低木 **44.** shrub
シダ **45.** fern
植物 **46.** plant
サボテン **47.** cactus-cacti
つる植物 **48.** vine
草 **49.** grass
ツタウルシ **50.** poison ivy

[11–22]
A. What kind of tree is that?
B. I think it's a/an ______ tree.

[31–48]
A. Look at all the ______s!
B. They're beautiful!

Describe your favorite tree and your favorite flower.
What kinds of trees and flowers grow where you live?

In your country, are flowers used at weddings? at funerals? on holidays? on visits to the hospital? Tell which flowers are used for different occasions.

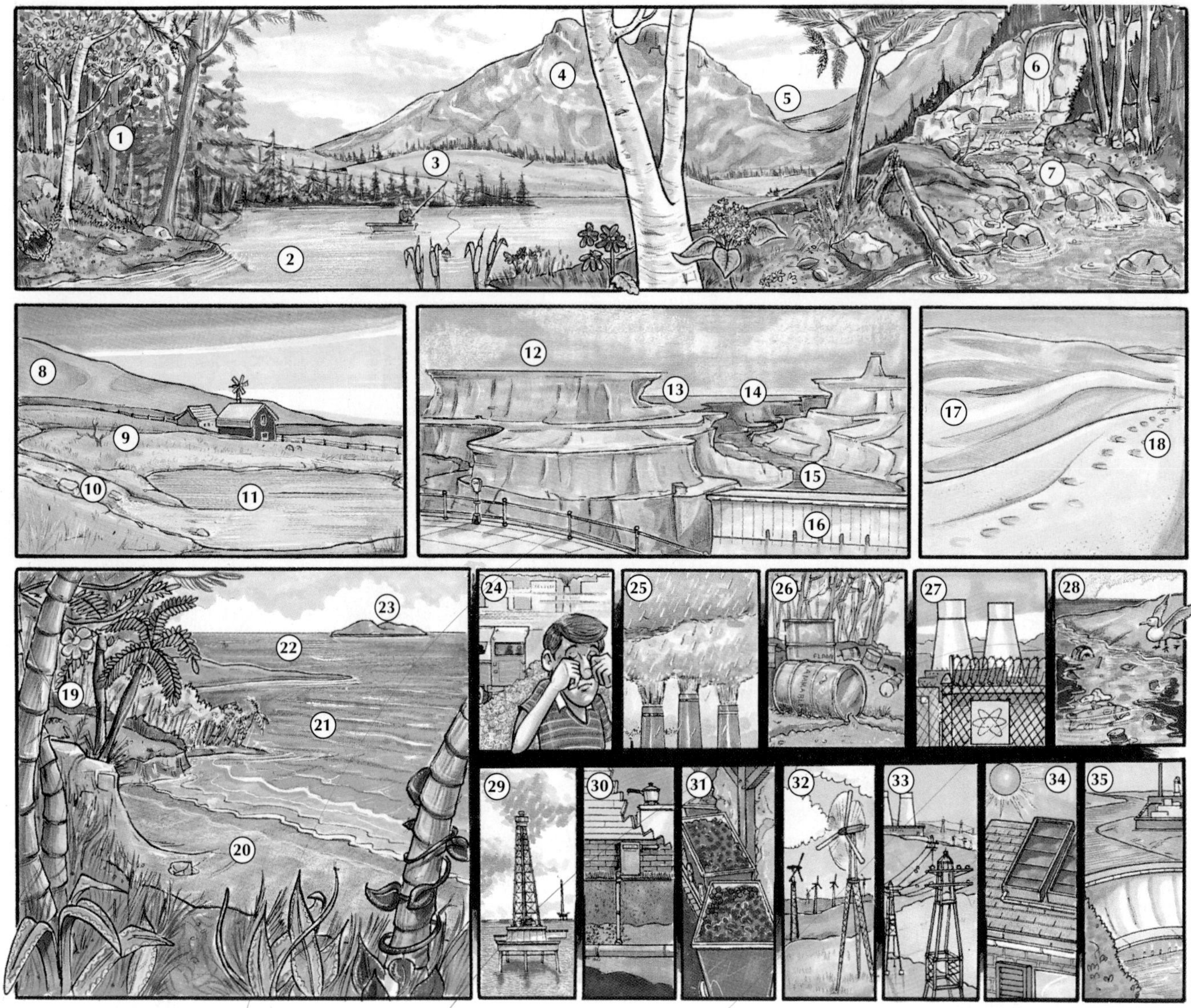

森林/森 **1.** forest/woods
湖 **2.** lake
草原 **3.** meadow
山 **4.** mountain
谷 **5.** valley
滝 **6.** waterfall
急流 **7.** rapids
丘 **8.** hill
野原 **9.** field
小川 **10.** stream/brook
池 **11.** pond
台地 **12.** plateau

がけ **13.** cliff
峡谷 **14.** canyon
川 **15.** river
ダム **16.** dam
砂漠 **17.** desert
砂丘 **18.** dune
ジャングル **19.** jungle
海岸 **20.** seashore
入り江 **21.** bay
海 **22.** ocean
島 **23.** island
大気汚染 **24.** air pollution

酸性雨 **25.** acid rain
有毒廃棄物 **26.** toxic waste
放射能 **27.** radiation
水質汚濁 **28.** water pollution
石油 **29.** oil
天然ガス **30.** (natural) gas
石炭 **31.** coal
風力 **32.** wind
核エネルギー/原子力 **33.** nuclear energy
太陽エネルギー **34.** solar energy
水力発電 **35.** hydroelectric power

[1–23]
A. { Isn't this a beautiful ________?!
Aren't these beautiful ________?!
B. It's/They're magnificent.

[24–28] A. Do you worry about the environment?
B. Yes. I'm very concerned about ________.

Describe some places of natural beauty in your country.

What kind of energy do you use to heat your home? to cook?
In your opinion, which kind of energy is best for producing electricity?

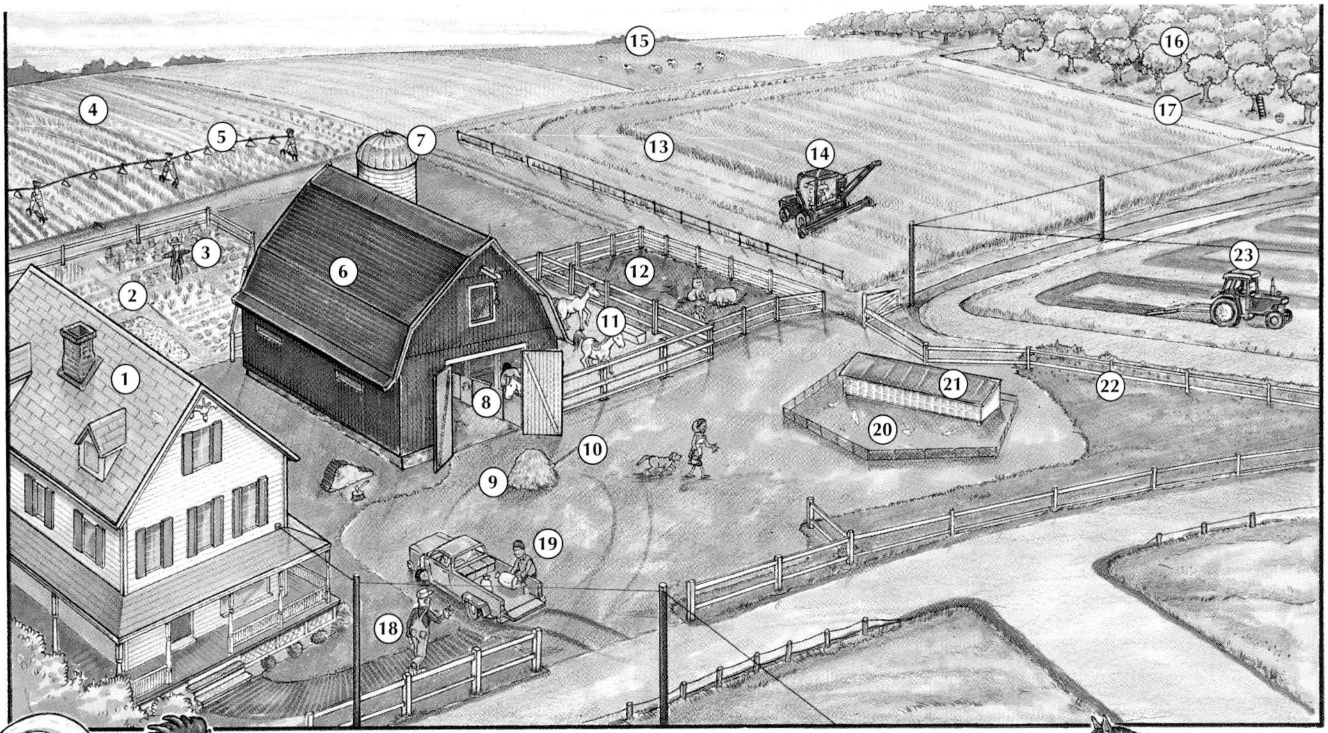

農家	**1.** farmhouse	コンバイン	**14.** combine	ヒヨコ	**26.** chick
野菜畑	**2.** (vegetable) garden	放牧場	**15.** pasture	七面鳥	**27.** turkey
カカシ	**3.** scarecrow	果樹園	**16.** orchard	ヤギ	**28.** goat
作物	**4.** crop	果樹	**17.** fruit tree	子ヤギ	**29.** kid
かんがい装置	**5.** irrigation system	農場主	**18.** farmer	羊	**30.** sheep
納屋	**6.** barn	作男	**19.** hired hand	子羊	**31.** lamb
サイロ	**7.** silo	ニワトリ飼育場	**20.** chicken coop	雄牛	**32.** bull
家畜小屋	**8.** stable	ニワトリ小屋	**21.** hen house	乳牛	**33.** (dairy) cow
干し草	**9.** hay	さく	**22.** fence	子牛	**34.** calf-calves
三つまた	**10.** pitchfork	トラクター	**23.** tractor	馬	**35.** horse
納屋の庭	**11.** barnyard	雄鶏	**24.** rooster	豚	**36.** pig
豚飼育場	**12.** pig pen/pig sty	ニワトリ	**25.** chicken/hen	子豚	**37.** piglet
畑	**13.** field				

A. Where's the ______?
B. In/On/Next to the ______.

A. The [24–37]s got loose again!
B. Oh, no! Where are they?
A. They're in the [1, 2, 12, 13, 15, 16, 20, 21]!

Tell about farms in your country.
What crops and animals are common on these farms?

キツネ	**1.** fox
ヤマアラシ	**2.** porcupine
針/とげ	**a.** quill
アライグマ	**3.** raccoon
オオカミ	**4.** wolf-wolves
ムース（アメリカヘラジカ）	**5.** moose
枝角	**a.** antler
シカ	**6.** deer
ひづめ	**a.** hoof
子ジカ	**7.** fawn
ハツカネズミ	**8.** mouse-mice
シマリス	**9.** chipmunk
野ネズミ	**10.** rat
リス	**11.** squirrel
ウサギ	**12.** rabbit
地リス	**13.** gopher
ビーバー	**14.** beaver
コウモリ	**15.** bat
スカンク	**16.** skunk
フクロネズミ	**17.** possum
ロバ	**18.** donkey
バッファロー	**19.** buffalo
ラクダ	**20.** camel
こぶ	**a.** hump
ラマ	**21.** llama
馬	**22.** horse
しっぽ	**a.** tail
子馬	**23.** foal
ポニー	**24.** pony
アルマジロ	**25.** armadillo
カンガルー	**26.** kangaroo
袋	**a.** pouch
ヒョウ	**27.** leopard
はん点	**a.** spots
キリン	**28.** giraffe
バイソン/野牛	**29.** bison
ゾウ	**30.** elephant
きば	**a.** tusk
（ゾウの）鼻	**b.** trunk
トラ	**31.** tiger
足	**a.** paw
ライオン	**32.** lion
たてがみ	**a.** mane
カバ	**33.** hippopotamus
ハイエナ	**34.** hyena
サイ	**35.** rhinoceros
角	**a.** horn
シマウマ	**36.** zebra
しま	**a.** stripes

クロクマ **37.** black bear
かぎづめ **a.** claw
ハイイログマ **38.** grizzly bear
シロクマ **39.** polar bear
コアラ **40.** koala (bear)
パンダ **41.** panda
サル **42.** monkey
チンパンジー **43.** chimpanzee

テナガザル **44.** gibbon
ヒヒ **45.** baboon
オランウータン **46.** orangutan
ゴリラ **47.** gorilla
アリクイ **48.** anteater
ミミズ **49.** worm
ナメクジ **50.** slug

ペット **Pets**
ネコ **51.** cat
（ネコ・ネズミなどの）ひげ **a.** whiskers
子ネコ **52.** kitten
犬 **53.** dog
子犬 **54.** puppy
ハムスター **55.** hamster
アレチネズミ **56.** gerbil
テンジクネズミ（モルモット） **57.** guinea pig

[1–50] A. Look at that ________!
B. Wow! That's the biggest ________ I've ever seen!

[51–57] A. Do you have a pet?
B. Yes. I have a ________.
A. What's your ________'s name?
B. …………

What animals can be found where you live?
Is there a zoo near where you live? What animals does the zoo have?
What are some common pets in your country?

If you were an animal, which animal do you think you would be? Why?
Does your culture have any popular folk tales or children's stories about animals? Tell a story you are familiar with.

鳥類 **A. Birds**

コマドリ **1.** robin
巣 **a.** nest
卵 **b.** egg
アオカケス **2.** blue jay
翼 **a.** wing
尾 **b.** tail
羽 **c.** feather
コウカンチョウ **3.** cardinal
ハチドリ **4.** hummingbird
キジ **5.** pheasant
カラス **6.** crow
カモメ **7.** seagull
スズメ **8.** sparrow
キツツキ **9.** woodpecker
くちばし **a.** beak
ツバメ **10.** swallow
ハト **11.** pigeon
フクロウ **12.** owl
タカ **13.** hawk
ワシ **14.** eagle
かぎづめ **a.** claw
カナリア **15.** canary
(冠毛のある)オウム **16.** cockatoo
オウム(インコを含む) **17.** parrot
インコ **18.** parakeet
カモ/アヒル **19.** duck
くちばし **a.** bill
子ガモ/アヒルの子 **20.** duckling
ガチョウ **21.** goose
ハクチョウ **22.** swan
フラミンゴ **23.** flamingo
ツル **24.** crane
コウノトリ **25.** stork
ペリカン **26.** pelican
クジャク **27.** peacock
ペンギン **28.** penguin
ミチバシリ **29.** roadrunner
ダチョウ **30.** ostrich

昆虫 **B. Insects**

ハエ **31.** fly
カ **32.** mosquito
ノミ **33.** flea
ホタル **34.** firefly/lightning bug
ガ **35.** moth
トンボ **36.** dragonfly
クモ **37.** spider
クモの巣 **a.** web
テントウムシ **38.** ladybug
スズメバチ **39.** wasp
ダニ **40.** tick
ハチ **41.** bee
ハチの巣 **a.** beehive
イモムシ/毛虫 **42.** caterpillar
まゆ **a.** cocoon
チョウ **43.** butterfly
バッタ **44.** grasshopper
アリ **45.** ant
カブトムシ **46.** beetle
シロアリ **47.** termite
ゴキブリ **48.** roach/cockroach
サソリ **49.** scorpion
ムカデ **50.** centipede
カマキリ **51.** praying mantis
コオロギ **52.** cricket

[1–52] A. Is that a/an _______?
B. No. I think it's a/an _______.

[31–52] A. Hold still! There's a _______ on your shirt!
B. Oh! Can you get it off of me?
A. There! It's gone!

What birds and insects can be found where you live?

Does your culture have any popular folk tales or children's stories about birds or insects? Tell a story you are familiar with.

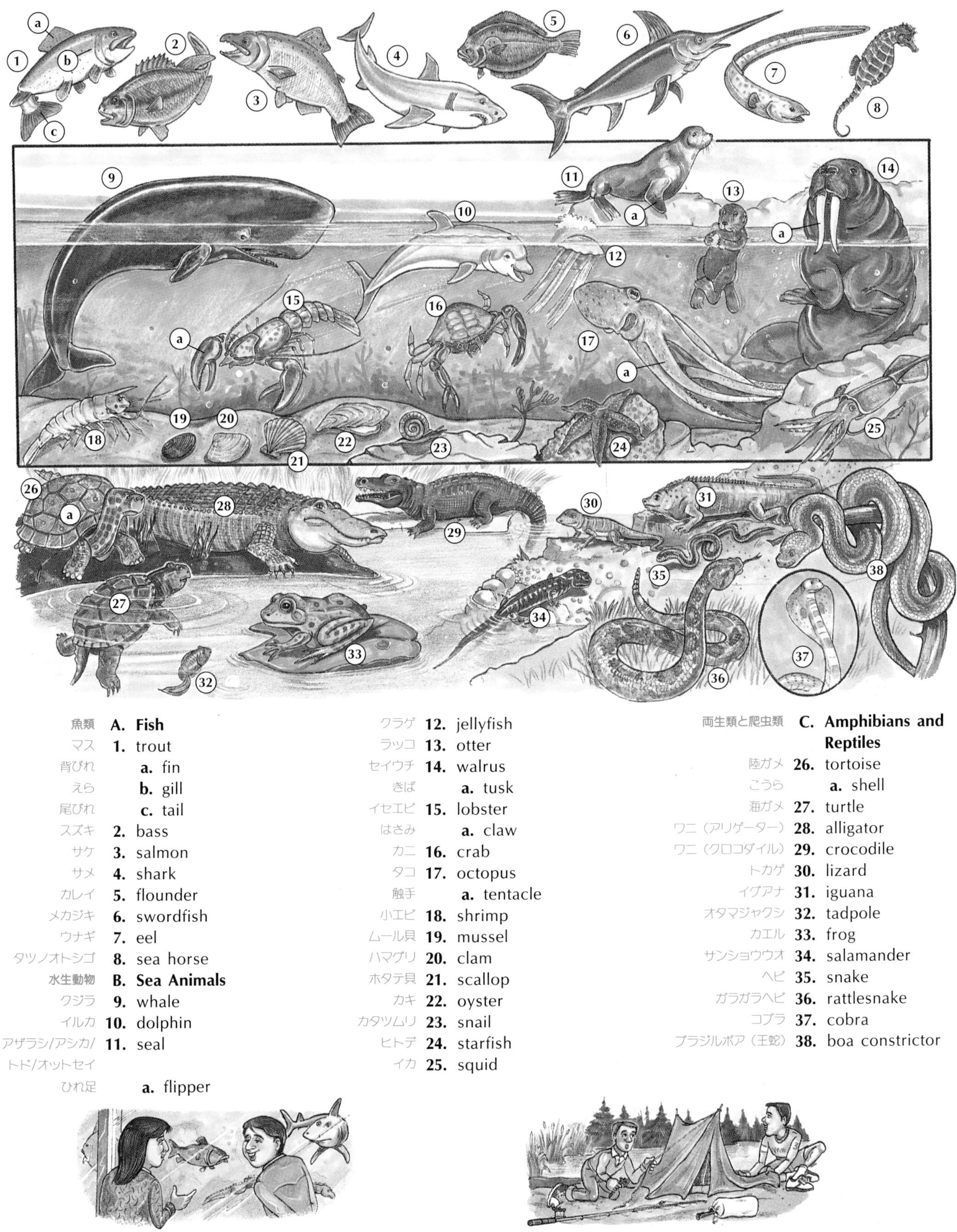

魚類 **A. Fish**
- マス **1.** trout
  - 背びれ **a.** fin
  - えら **b.** gill
  - 尾びれ **c.** tail
- スズキ **2.** bass
- サケ **3.** salmon
- サメ **4.** shark
- カレイ **5.** flounder
- メカジキ **6.** swordfish
- ウナギ **7.** eel
- タツノオトシゴ **8.** sea horse

水生動物 **B. Sea Animals**
- クジラ **9.** whale
- イルカ **10.** dolphin
- アザラシ/アシカ/トド/オットセイ **11.** seal
  - ひれ足 **a.** flipper
- クラゲ **12.** jellyfish
- ラッコ **13.** otter
- セイウチ **14.** walrus
  - きば **a.** tusk
- イセエビ **15.** lobster
  - はさみ **a.** claw
- カニ **16.** crab
- タコ **17.** octopus
  - 触手 **a.** tentacle
- 小エビ **18.** shrimp
- ムール貝 **19.** mussel
- ハマグリ **20.** clam
- ホタテ貝 **21.** scallop
- カキ **22.** oyster
- カタツムリ **23.** snail
- ヒトデ **24.** starfish
- イカ **25.** squid

両生類と爬虫類 **C. Amphibians and Reptiles**
- 陸ガメ **26.** tortoise
  - こうら **a.** shell
- 海ガメ **27.** turtle
- ワニ（アリゲーター） **28.** alligator
- ワニ（クロコダイル） **29.** crocodile
- トカゲ **30.** lizard
- イグアナ **31.** iguana
- オタマジャクシ **32.** tadpole
- カエル **33.** frog
- サンショウウオ **34.** salamander
- ヘビ **35.** snake
- ガラガラヘビ **36.** rattlesnake
- コブラ **37.** cobra
- ブラジルボア（王蛇） **38.** boa constrictor

[1–38] A. Is that a/an ________?
B. No. I think it's a/an ________.

[26–38] A. Are there any ________s around here?
B. No. But there are lots of ________s.

What fish, sea animals, and reptiles can be found in your country? Which ones are endangered and need to be protected? Why?

In your opinion, which ones are the most interesting? the most beautiful? the most dangerous?

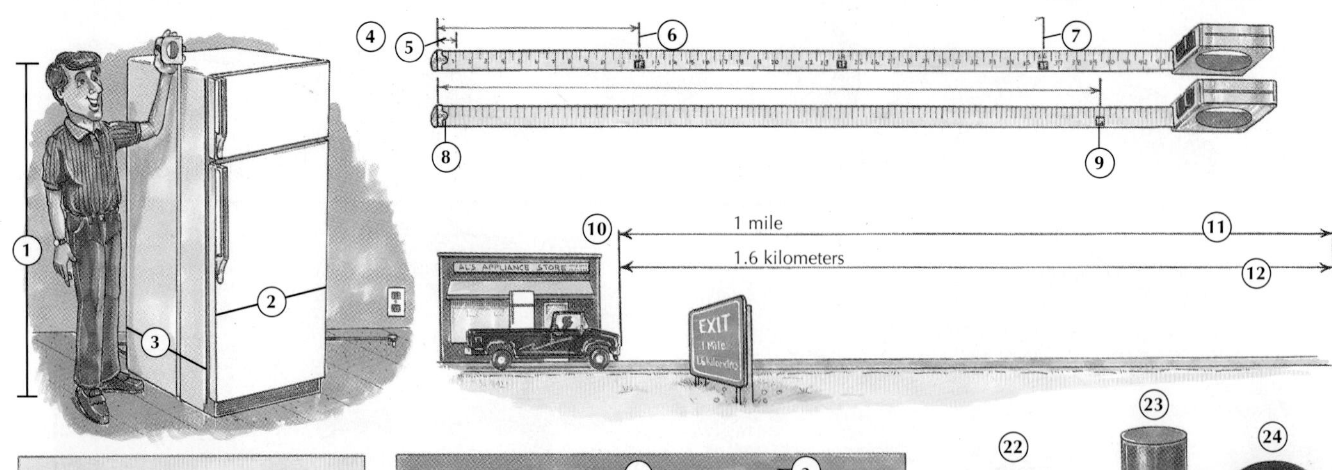

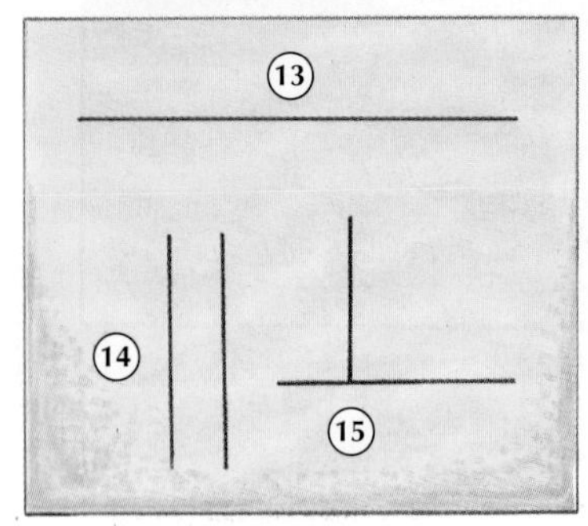

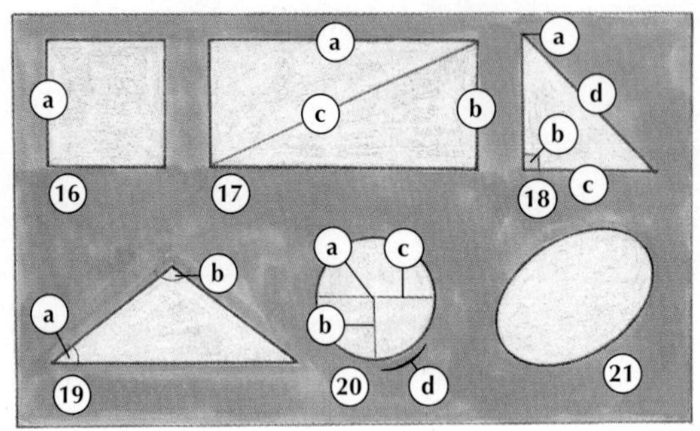

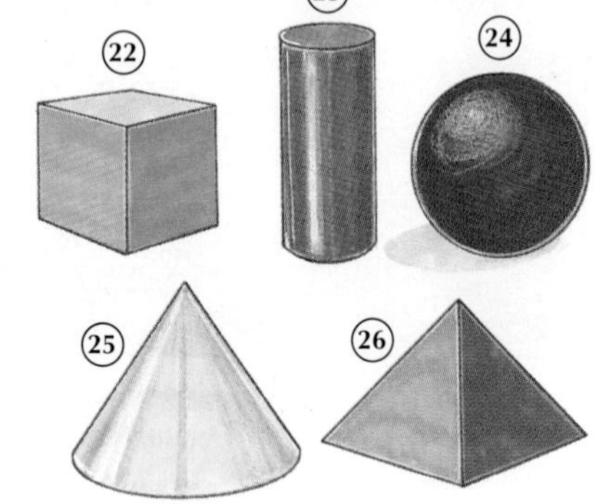

寸法 **A. Measurements**
高さ **1.** height
幅 **2.** width
奥行き **3.** depth
長さ **4.** length
インチ **5.** inch
フットｰフィート **6.** foot-feet
ヤード **7.** yard
センチメートル **8.** centimeter
メートル **9.** meter
距離 **10.** distance
マイル **11.** mile
キロメートル **12.** kilometer
線 **B. Lines**
直線 **13.** straight line
平行線 **14.** parallel lines
垂直線 **15.** perpendicular lines
幾何図形 **C. Geometric Shapes**
正方形 **16.** square
辺 **a.** side
長方形 **17.** rectangle
たて **a.** length
よこ **b.** width
対角線 **c.** diagonal
直角三角形 **18.** right triangle
頂点 **a.** apex
直角 **b.** right angle
底辺 **c.** base
斜辺 **d.** hypotenuse
二等辺三角形 **19.** isosceles triangle
鋭角 **a.** acute angle
鈍角 **b.** obtuse angle
円 **20.** circle
中心 **a.** center
半径 **b.** radius
直径 **c.** diameter
円周 **d.** circumference
だ円 **21.** ellipse/oval
立体図形 **D. Solid Figures**
立方体 **22.** cube
円柱 **23.** cylinder
球 **24.** sphere
円すい **25.** cone
角すい **26.** pyramid

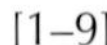

[1–9]
A. What's the [1–4] ?
B. .... [5–9] (s).

[11–12]
A. What's the distance?
B. .... ________(s).

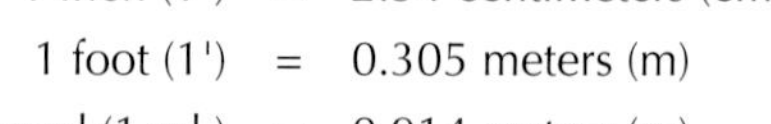

1 inch (1")	=	2.54 centimeters (cm)
1 foot (1')	=	0.305 meters (m)
1 yard (1 yd.)	=	0.914 meters (m)
1 mile (mi.)	=	1.6 kilometers (km)

[16–21]
A. Who can tell me what shape this is?
B. I can. It's a/an ________.

[22–26]
A. Who knows what figure this is?
B. I do. It's a/an ________.

[13–26]
A. This painting is magnificent!
B. Hmm. I don't think so. It just looks like a lot of ________s and ________s to me!

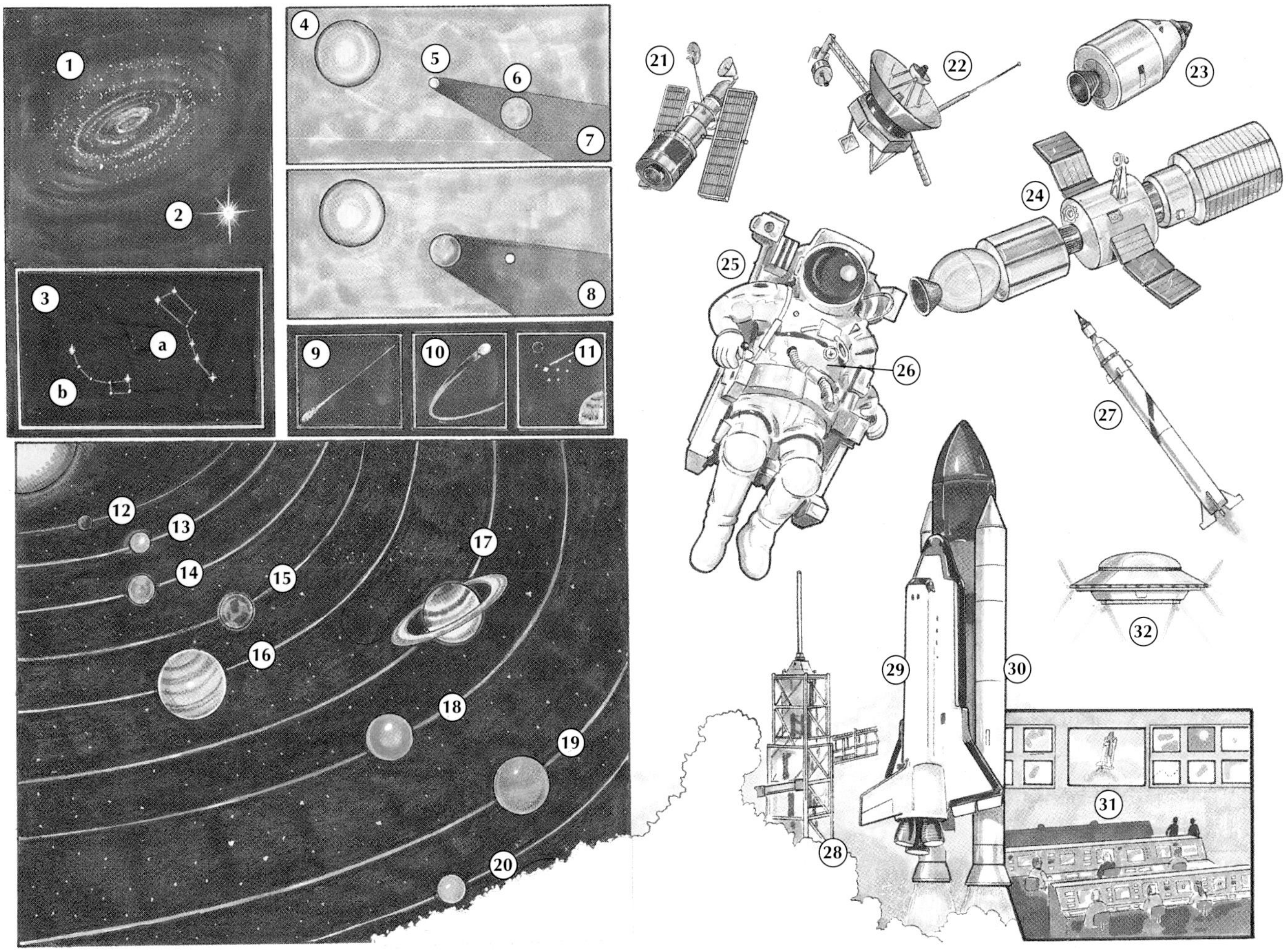

宇宙 A. The Universe

- 星雲 **1.** galaxy
- 星 **2.** star
- 星座 **3.** constellation
  - 北斗七星 **a.** The Big Dipper
  - 小熊座の小びしゃく **b.** The Little Dipper

太陽系 B. The Solar System

- 太陽 **4.** sun
- 月 **5.** moon
- 惑星 **6.** planet
- 日食 **7.** solar eclipse
- 月食 **8.** lunar eclipse
- 流れ星 **9.** meteor
- すい星 **10.** comet
- 小惑星 **11.** asteroid
- 水星 **12.** Mercury
- 金星 **13.** Venus
- 地球 **14.** Earth
- 火星 **15.** Mars
- 木星 **16.** Jupiter
- 土星 **17.** Saturn
- 天王星 **18.** Uranus
- 海王星 **19.** Neptune
- 冥めい王星 **20.** Pluto

宇宙探検 C. Space Exploration

- 人工衛星 **21.** satellite
- 宇宙観測機 **22.** (space) probe
- 宇宙船/人工衛星 **23.** space craft/orbiter
- 宇宙ステーション **24.** space station
- 宇宙飛行士 **25.** astronaut
- 宇宙服 **26.** space suit
- ロケット **27.** rocket
- ロケット発射台 **28.** launch pad
- スペースシャトル **29.** space shuttle
- ブースターロケット/補助推進ロケット **30.** booster rocket
- （地上の）宇宙管制センター **31.** mission control
- UFO/未確認飛行物体/空飛ぶ円盤 **32.** U.F.O./Unidentified Flying Object/flying saucer

[1–20]

A. Is that (a/an/the) ________?

B. I'm not sure. I think it might be (a/an/the) ________.

[21–27, 29, 31]

A. Is the ________ ready for tomorrow's launch?

B. Yes. "All systems are go!"

Pretend you are an astronaut traveling in space. What do you see?

Draw and name a constellation you are familiar with.

Do you think space exploration is important? Why?

Have you ever seen a U.F.O.? Do you believe there is life in outer space? Why?

索引の見方：太い数字は単語の掲載ページを示し、右側の細い数字はそのページの上のイラスト番号および単語リスト番号を示しています。例えば、"north **5**-1" は、*north* という単語が5ページの項目１に掲載されていることを意味します。

Cardinal Numbers 30

1	one
2	two
3	three
4	four
5	five
6	six
7	seven
8	eight
9	nine
10	ten
11	eleven
12	twelve
13	thirteen
14	fourteen
15	fifteen
16	sixteen
17	seventeen
18	eighteen
19	nineteen
20	twenty
21	twenty-one
22	twenty-two
30	thirty
40	forty
50	fifty
60	sixty
70	seventy
80	eighty
90	ninety
100	one hundred
101	one hundred (and) one
102	one hundred (and) two
1,000	one thousand
10,000	ten thousand
100,000	one hundred thousand
1,000,000	one million

Ordinal Numbers 30

1st	first
2nd	second
3rd	third
4th	fourth
5th	fifth
6th	sixth
7th	seventh
8th	eighth
9th	ninth
10th	tenth
11th	eleventh
12th	twelfth
13th	thirteenth
14th	fourteenth
15th	fifteenth
16th	sixteenth
17th	seventeenth
18th	eighteenth
19th	nineteenth
20th	twentieth
21st	twenty-first
22nd	twenty-second
30th	thirtieth
40th	fortieth
50th	fiftieth
60th	sixtieth
70th	seventieth
80th	eightieth
90th	ninetieth
100th	one hundredth
101st	one hundred (and) first
102nd	one hundred (and) second
1,000th	one thousandth
10,000th	ten thousandth
100,000th	one hundred thousandth
1,000,000th	one millionth

Days of the Week 33

Sunday
Monday
Tuesday
Wednesday
Thursday
Friday
Saturday

Months of the Year 33

January
February
March
April
May
June
July
August
September
October
November
December